Dignity in America

Dignity in America

Transforming Social Conflicts

ERIN DALY

STANFORD UNIVERSITY PRESS
Stanford, California

Stanford University Press
Stanford, California

Library of Congress Cataloging-in-Publication Data

Names: Daly, Erin, author.
Title: Dignity in America : transforming social conflicts / Erin Daly.
Description: Stanford, California : Stanford University Press, 2025. |
    Includes bibliographical references and index.
Identifiers: LCCN 2024041830 (print) | LCCN 2024041831 (ebook) |
    ISBN 9781503642171 (cloth) | ISBN 9781503642188 (paperback) |
    ISBN 9781503642782 (ebook)
Subjects: LCSH: Respect for persons—Law and legislation—United
    States. | Human rights—United States. | Civil rights—United
    States. | Dignity—Political aspects—United States. | Social
    conflict—United States.
Classification: LCC KF4766 .D35 2025 (print) | LCC KF4766 (ebook) |
    DDC 323.0973—dc23/eng/20240909
LC record available at https://lccn.loc.gov/2024041830
LC ebook record available at https://lccn.loc.gov/2024041831

Cover design: Derek Thornton / Notch Design

The authorized representative in the EU for product safety
and compliance is: Mare Nostrum Group B.V. | Mauritskade
21D | 1091 GC Amsterdam | The Netherlands | Email address:
gpsr@mare-nostrum.co.uk | KVK chamber of commerce
number: 96249943

"We must define democracy as that form of government and of society which is inspired above every other with the feeling and consciousness of the dignity of man."

— Thomas Mann, *The Magic Mountain*

"The American Bar Association has resolved that 'Human dignity — the inherent, equal, and inalienable worth of every person — is foundational to a just rule of law;' and 'urges governments to ensure that 'dignity rights' – the principle that human dignity is fundamental to all areas of law and policy — be reflected in the exercise of their legislative, executive, and judicial functions.'"

— American Bar Association Resolution, 2019

Contents

PREFACE

What Is Dignity, and
Why Does It Matter Now?

Dignity is the essential quality that makes each of us value our own life. It's how we know we are important. And it's how we know everyone else is equally important. Every life matters. And *that* matters now for two central reasons.

First, human dignity matters because it matters to people. People have a sense of their own dignity, their own self-worth. And for most people, that makes them want to be treated with respect, "as a person," not as something less, like an object or an animal. It makes them want to protect their individuality and live their life according to their desires and needs. And when that doesn't happen—when people are hurt or humiliated or denied or deprived of something—it's their dignity that gets hurt. So they want to make things right. Dignity is what fuels people's sense of justice. People don't complain because section 123(a) of some statute was violated. They complain because their dignity was harmed in some perhaps inarticulable way. But it's enough to galvanize them to redress, to sue, to fight, to take to the streets, to tell their story. The desire to live with dignity is how people measure their own sense of well-being and their sense of justice.

But it's not just some inchoate sense of well-being or, in its absence, some vague sense that something is wrong in the world. It may be "a difficult-to-define term, one that is leveraged to win arguments," as Steven Hitlin and Matthew A. Andersson say in *The Science of Dignity*, but I believe it has substance, and contours, and power, and limits, and it can be used not just to win arguments but to advance social justice so that more people can live happier and more fulfilling lives. We know this because courts around the world are using the concept of human dignity in just this way: to protect rights, to limit governmental power, and to preserve and protect what is "sacred" about every human life. They are defining dignity with clarity and specificity and showing why and how it's relevant in the concrete settings of court cases.

And that is the second reason why dignity matters now. Dignity has become the axis around which human rights law— and perhaps all law—revolves. Since the Universal Declaration of Human Rights (UDHR) was adopted by the United Nations more than seventy-five years ago, the "inherent dignity" of the human person has been both the foundation and the purpose of human rights, their alpha and their omega. Indeed, the UDHR went even further, betting the whole game on dignity: the preamble affirms that the "inherent dignity and . . . the equal and inalienable rights of all members of the human family is the foundation of freedom, justice and peace in the world"—a heavy burden for the simple idea of dignity to bear!

Since then, the idea of human dignity has spread not only throughout international and regional human rights law but also to the constitutions of almost every country on earth. The Basic Law of Germany affirms that "human dignity is inviolable" and insists that "to respect and protect it shall be the duty of all state authority." The Constitution of Peru makes it the very purpose of the state: "The defense of the human person and respect for his dignity are the supreme purpose of the society and the State" (Art. 1). The Philippines Constitution assures that "the State values the dignity of every human person and guarantees full respect for human rights" (Art. II, Principles, Sec. 11). In Kenya, "The purpose of recognising and protecting human rights and fundamental freedoms is to preserve the dignity of individuals and communities and to promote social justice and the realisation of the potential of all human beings" (Chap. 4, Pt. 1.19.2). These are just a few examples drawn from more than 170 constitutions that refer to human dignity. And now the courts of many of these countries have taken hold of these constitutional mandates and developed a robust jurisprudence of dignity rights. These cases have realigned our thinking about what entitlements people have just by virtue of having been born human and the role of government in protecting those entitlements.

People organize their lives and their value systems around their own sense of dignity, and they want to live in a society that aligns with those values and protects their worth as human beings. In that way, the idea of dignity is intimately linked to our idea of government and our conceptions of society in general. Some people want the government to provide things like housing and health care in order to protect their dignity. Others think their dignity will be best protected if the government stays out of their way (though, as we will see, most Americans still want health care, a proper response to climate change, and protection of their rights). Whatever you want the government to do or not do, it probably comes down to how you think government will best protect what's most important to you, and that's probably your own sense of your self-worth and the value of your life. So we should be asking: What do we want for ourselves? What do we owe to each other?

We can use the concept of dignity to think through these questions and decide what kinds of policies we want and how we want the government to act in the face of need, crisis, and injustices of all kinds. This book aims to start us on our way by showing how we can transform social conflicts through dignity. This book addresses many of the most complex, perplexing, and persistent challenges facing Americans today. But it does so without any pretense of providing the kind of detailed or in-depth expert analysis that each issue is due. The aim here is much narrower. In these pages, I look at these issues through a lens of human dignity. The discussion is limited to showing how these situations—whether climate change or poverty or the denial of the right to vote—impact people's dignity and how, by reshaping the terms of debate, we can develop policies that will enable more people to live with greater dignity.

Throughout the world, the idea of dignity is taking hold as a barometer of human well-being. Courts have been at the forefront of this movement: in the last few decades, there has been a veritable explosion of cases from every corner of the world that define, elucidate, and apply the idea of human dignity, sometimes to hold governments accountable to established standards, sometimes as a transformative tool, to goad them into doing more than they have in the past. Dignity matters, these courts are saying, and our laws and public policies should protect it.

In the United States, there are sporadic suggestions that human dignity is the litmus test for what we think the government should or should not do, but the language of dignity is not nearly as deeply rooted here as it is elsewhere. The US Supreme Court has explained, for example, that we protect the freedom of expression in order to "remove governmental restraints from the arena of public discussion, putting the decision as to what views shall be voiced largely into the hands of each of us, in the hope that use of such freedom will ultimately produce a more capable citizenry and more perfect polity and in the belief that no other approach would comport with the premise of individual dignity and choice upon which our political system rests."[1] We allow a broad and active marketplace of ideas because it's a matter of human dignity, not the prerogative of government to decide what people can say, what they can hear, or what they can believe. It's up to us—as a matter of our own worth—to decide what to do with the information we get. On the issue of marriage, the Supreme Court said simply that those who seek to have their same-sex marriages recognized "ask for equal dignity in the eyes of the law. The Constitution grants them that right."[2] And, in an oft-repeated phrase, the Court has said that the Eighth Amendment's protection against cruel and unusual punishment is "about nothing less than the dignity of man."[3]

Despite these notable pronouncements, the US Supreme Court has never really embraced a jurisprudence of dignity. This makes it somewhat of an outlier in the modern world: courts from Peru to Pakistan, from Slovenia to South Africa, have committed to the idea of dignity as a foundational value and an actionable right, as have tribunals at the regional levels in Europe, Africa, and the Americas, as well as at the highest levels of international law. Even the United States has adopted it as a goal at the international level: the New Atlantic Charter, signed in 2021 by the president of the United States and the prime minister of the United Kingdom, "reaffirm[s] their commitment to work together to realise our vision for a more peaceful and prosperous future" by resolving, first, to "defend the inherent dignity and human rights of all individuals."[4] However, for a variety of reasons, the US courts have not done so and do not seem poised to do so anytime soon. But the Supreme Court is not the only decision-maker around. And in a democracy, it is not even the most important one. We, the people, are.

So this book does not make legal or jurisprudential arguments intended to persuade a court to make a commitment to dignity (though it would be wonderful if it accomplished that). At most, it uses the courts' jurisprudence as an authoritative pronouncement or explanation of certain issues: how we are supposed to think about affirmative action or the right to privacy or freedom of speech. At times it embraces the language a court has used to get at the themes of human dignity, and at times it points to opportunities that the courts have missed to protect human dignity. But the argument is not primarily to the courts. Rather, it's to *we the people.*

It is the hope of this book that we, the people, will approach our seemingly intractable social conflicts and develop thoughtful policies for our nation through the prism of human dignity. In this way, we can tell our government and our courts that we want to live in a world where people treat each other with dignity and where we can all live with dignity.

We might think of this perspective—what might be called the politics of dignity in counterposition to the politics of fear, which seems to be in ascendancy in some parts. Because the politics of dignity is built on the idea of each person's equal and intrinsic value, it approaches social problems from a perspective of human development and inclusion and seeks to find ways to ensure that all people have the equal entitlement to and capability of living their life to the fullest. A politics of fear, on the other hand, treats others as a threat to, different from, or less than one another. It separates people from each other, whether through border walls or prison bars or less explicitly by entrenching poverty and reifying social hierarchies. It limits opportunities for inclusion through public services like education and health care. It prefers the idea of supremacy among human beings to inherent equality of "all members of the human family." It depletes the space in which democracy happens and rule of law governs, to expand rule by power and force.

The politics of dignity is grounded in a view of human nature that is egalitarian and inclusive and a view of the future that is optimistic. It imagines that America can support and protect the essential humanity of each person within our large and colorful community. It seeks to transform social conflicts into quests for dignity.

But what would that look like? How can we insist on a politics that really protects the value of each person's life? How can we try to figure out the most vexing problems of our day by recourse to this commitment? How can we use it as our lodestar to guide us toward solutions that allow more people to live each day with more dignity?

This book examines these questions. It is based on a hunch and is motivated by a desire to explore whether that hunch is true. The hunch is that the promise of human dignity can help us work toward better solutions for the nation's most pressing problems. The book isn't left or right, not pro-this or anti-that. It doesn't advocate for a particular political outcome. It's not about partisan politics. It's about asking a simple question: What would society look like if policies were designed to respect, protect, and promote each person's inherent and equal worth?

We start with a working definition of human dignity. This is more challenging than it seems at first blush, for two opposing reasons. Even though we all have an intuitive sense of what dignity means, it can be hard to put it into words, so there is no clear working definition of dignity. The law does not give us a precise definition of dignity at either the international or domestic level. Still, when courts and tribunals and treaties and constitutions talk about human dignity, they use the term in startlingly similar ways. There is, in other words, a very strong global consensus about what human dignity means and why it's important. I think that's because when they talk about dignity, they are not talking about something that's particular to their legal culture or tradition; rather, they are talking about what it means to be a human being in the twenty-first century.[5] This global consensus, which transcends culture and spans geography, can be described as three baskets of interests or needs, defined by an overarching principle.

First, people want to have some control over their lives and to be able to make decisions for themselves and experience life as they choose and fully and freely develop their personality. We can call this the "personhood" principle of dignity. Second, they want to be treated with dignity by others: that is, with respect for their own worth as human beings. This "humanity" principle recognizes that no one wants to be humiliated or demeaned or treated as "less than" a human being. And third, people want to be able to live with dignity; that is, they want to be able to live decently. The "decency" principle is going to apply differently for different people in different places and cultures. But everyone wants to live with adequate shelter and be protected from the elements, with enough nutritious food and clean water so they can live and stay healthy, and with opportunities for engagement on an equal footing in community with others.

These are some of the basic elements that courts talk about when they describe human dignity. Notice that these three principles are interrelated and, in some ways, even indivisible. You can't control the course of your life if you don't have enough to eat and don't have clean water, which limits the way you participate in your community, which affects the way people treat you. And so on. We will explore these premises more in Chapter 1 and draw on them throughout the book.

The remaining chapters of the book apply these principles to help us reach better resolutions to some of the nation's most important and intractable public issues. Using dignity in this way doesn't necessarily tell us how to resolve the problems—whether abortion or affirmative action should be constitutional or what to do about homelessness or how to mitigate climate change—because we may have different social and personal priorities and points of view. We do not all have to agree on how to live the good life. But we might start by agreeing that laws and government action should be directed toward enhancing each person's ability to define the good life for themselves. And that is the essence of human dignity.

So dignity is all over the place. (As you read this book, you will start to notice it more in everyday life.) It's in each of us. I think it resides somewhere between the gut and the heart, but you may locate it elsewhere, or not at all in the body. And it's in our sense of justice. It's a useful concept to help us define the kind of society we want. So let's pay attention to it. Let's take it seriously.

AUTHOR'S STATEMENT

This book offers a way to think about the problems that face America through the lens of human dignity. The basic argument is that if we aim to be a country in which more people can live more fulfilling lives, be secure in their own inherent sense of dignity, and treat all others with equal dignity, we solve a lot of the most pressing issues facing America in the early 21st century. Living with dignity should be our north star.

The foundation for this approach is the commitment that the world made in the wake of the second world war to reaffirm "faith" in the equal and inherent dignity of "every member of the human family," to quote the Universal Declaration of Human Rights. It *is* a matter of faith because of course we don't know. But after the "untold sorrows" that two world wars brought, a community of people came together to form the United Nations in the belief that faith in equal dignity of all people was a more secure basis for a common future than any alternative.

That faith is enduring.

Human dignity remains the same as it has been since the dawn of humankind, since humans first became self-aware, first started to think about their interactions with other humans and with the environment around them, first started to communicate their thoughts and ideas with each other, first started to feel empathy toward others, and deserving of respect from others. Human dignity is the simple signifier for a very complex set of notions – that we humans, uniquely, have the capacity for reflection and self-reflection, the inclination for creation and re-creation, the ability (and the choice) to be self-conscious and conscientious, the ability to be inspirational and aspirational. Dignity is the sense we have of ourselves in the world. It's the sense we have of the importance of our lives.

As author Glen Martin has written, the Universal Declaration's faith in human dignity "may well be the most important moral statement of the 20th century as well as the most widely influential." And none comes close in the 21st century so far.

But it is not just a moral tale. It's a political imperative. Of all the forms of government, only constitutional democracies reflect and promote human dignity. Democracies ensure that each one of us – *we the people* – make important decisions for ourselves rather than forfeiting that power to anyone else. Constitutionalism, moreover, ensures those decisions have guardrails – that no matter how many people want to or how much power those people have, they can never destroy the essential humanity of another person. Constitutions do this both by enumerating rights that people have, such as freedom of expression and association, equality, and certain fundamental liberties and by limiting the power of government in order to to protect the core values of personhood. Under the US Constitution, the federal government is empowered to act, but it may never, ever encroach on the integrity of any person. It must always respect the space in which people live as themselves and for themselves.

When we lose our commitment to human dignity, we enter into fields of authoritarianism and totalitarianism. Authoritarian governments are dangerous precisely because they erode the authority that each person has to make decisions for themselves. We call governments totalitarian when they threaten to totally usurp the agency that dignity gives each person to live life as they choose. These forms of government blur the boundary between the individual and the state, making the individual a pawn of the state. They encroach on the sphere of the human being, limiting the field of human development and individual authority. The use of human beings for slave labor, or for procreation are first and foremost violations of human dignity precisely because they fail to respect the authority of each person to live as a person. Indeed, as the Argentine Supreme Court has explained, "the protection of the scope of privacy ... is one of the greatest values of respect for the dignity of the human being and a feature of the essential difference between the rule of law and authoritarian forms of government."[a]

More recently, the Supreme Court of Puerto Rico explained the relationship between dignity and freedom in a 2019 decision involving compelled membership in a mechanics' union. Siding with the mechanics who did not want to be forced to join the union, the Court explained: "There is a basic interdependence among the human freedom, freedom from ignorance, freedom from fear, freedom to think freely, and freedom to speak, associate and assemble freely. All these freedoms, in fact, become the matrix where the human personality progresses to its fullest manifestation and where the essential dignity of the human being is attained."[b]

---

[a] Association for the struggle of Transvestite-Transexual Identity v. Inspector General of Justice, National Supreme Court of Justice (2006).

[b] Rodriguez Casillas v. Commonwealth, No. AC-2017-0076, 2019 PR Sup. LEXIS 79 (P.R. May 8, 2019).

I believe that the commitment to dignity is especially salient right now, as America is reckoning with its own democratic instincts. The two most important rights in our constitutional system are liberty and equality, both protected against incursions by the federal government and the states. Dignity is different from both, but it lies at the confluence of these two rivers of rights. To live with dignity is to have the freedom, or liberty, to live life on one's own terms. It is to be treated "as a person" always and never as anything less. It is different from liberty in that it not only suggests freedom *from* government incursion, but it claims rights to government protection and support as needed so that everyone can live with dignity.

At the same time, dignity is related to, but not identical to, equality. It is a right of inclusion and respect. It protects the equal right to make private decisions and to participate in public life on an equal basis with all others. When we commit to dignity, we ensure that everyone has the same rights as everyone else to protect their dignity and to claim their rights. Racism, nationalism, nativism, antisemitism, and sexism, like xeno-, homo-, and transphobia, as well as misogyny and supremacy – all gaining visibility in the present day – are fundamentally at odds with a dignity-based society in which all people are included on an equal basis in the human, social, and political community.

The faith in human dignity persists, even as we face ever more daunting challenges: democracies that are fraying and fragile, corporate power that seems to resist regulation, a planetary climate that is reaching its boiling point, wars that are changing the face of the earth, persistent and pervasive poverty in America and throughout the globe, and more.

This book assumes that Americans still want to live with dignity. We want safety and security, communities and families that bind people together, the ability to decide for ourselves how we want to be. We want to protect zones of privacy where we can live our lives without interference or control. We want our lives to matter, we want to be treated with respect, we want our children to have better lives, with more joy and fewer sorrows.

This book offers the hope that we can approach our national conflicts with the aim of accomplishing those goals. We could think about poverty, crime, and climate change in terms of human dignity. We could ensure that everyone has an equal voice because every person deserves to be heard. We could choose a politics of respect so that everyone in our American community can live equally full and dignified lives.

Dignity in America

ONE

What We Mean When We Talk about Dignity

The Essence of Suffering

Pick your favorite injustice. Anyone you want—war, genocide, mass incarceration, extreme poverty, misogyny, racism, . . . your choice. Now think about it for a moment. Why is it an injustice? Why is it painful to think about? Why do we want a world without war, where the climate doesn't turn people into refugees, where people with power don't abuse people without power, where people without power are not humiliated? Why do we aspire to a world without injustice?

Depending on which injustice you choose, the answers may vary, but they all come down to the same point: they are injustices because they make people suffer and we want people to not suffer. And the reason we want people to not suffer is that people—uniquely—have human dignity. Each life is sacred, each life is immeasurably valuable. We don't worry when a table is damaged or and we don't cry when a company files for bankruptcy, but we can be sad when a person hurts or dies. The very essence of suffering is the harm to a person's dignity. Beyond the scars left on the body, it's the hurt that sits somewhere between the heart and the gut that is the indignity we want to protect against. Now, we can debate (and people do) whether trees and dolphins and ecosystems and other living things have dignity, but we don't have to resolve those questions now: the only commitment that concerns us here is that human beings do have inherent value, human suffering should be reduced, and that demands action.

When we talk about injustices, of all kinds, and we try to develop good policies that will make the world a better place, we are implicitly doing this because we have an innate belief in the inherent and equal worth of every member of the human family.

Aiming for Dignity

Once we realize that indignity is the essence of injustice, we know exactly how to right the ship. We know that dignity and injustice are inversely related, that we reduce injustice as more people live happier, fuller lives. Now, of course, everyone has a different idea of what that means. For some people it's riding all day in a hot-air balloon. For others it's tilling the land. For some it's being a mom or a dad, and for others it's avoiding parenting. However we define it, to live with dignity is to be able to define it for oneself.

In advocating for the recognition of dignity "as a public health concern,"[1] Hitlin and Andersson take a subjective approach to define it:

> Like individuals deeming themselves as "happy" or as leading a "meaningful life," allowing individuals to interpret "dignity" for themselves—as individual, moral subjects—helps to circumvent philosophical, theoretical and legal debates about dignity's "true" meaning.[2]

This is consistent with the idea that dignity entails having agency over one's life, including the agency to decide the course of one's life for oneself. The global law builds on this insight. Dignity law does not tell people how to be happy or what it means to be happy. It describes the basic premises that people tend to agree on. It turns out that when you ask people what dignity means, even people from radically different cultures with radically different conceptions and ideas about the meaning of life, their answers are convergent. Courts have captured this global, human sense of dignity. It comes down to three essential aspirations.

First, people should be able to live according to their own sense of dignity, that is, according to their own chosen identity; they should not be forced to belong to a particular group or to identify with particular traits. If we think about Nazism, for instance, we notice that one way in which dignity was damaged was by identifying people as Jewish, whether or not they took on that identity for themselves. Jim Crow identified who was black by their bloodline, not by how they identified themselves. In the twenty-first century, we see this in issues of gender identity and sexual orientation. Oppressive laws define how people should identify *for* them, but courts that have considered these matters have tended to hold that people should be able to choose their identity for themselves, whether male or female or neither or a third gender or something else.

But it's not just about identity but also includes how we make decisions in our lives. To have dignity is to be able to make decisions for ourselves, to have agency over our own lives. Who else would we want to make decisions for us? Matthew McManus calls this "self-authorship."[3] Policies that force people into certain jobs or to or away from educational opportunities violate a person's dignity for this reason. Policies that compel or impede intimate relationships or child rearing violate human dignity because they treat people not as agents in their own right but as a means to someone else's end. In cases ranging from reproductive rights, to marriage, to the right to refuse medical treatment, and more, courts have found that each person should have control over their own life course. This aligns with the Supreme Court's protection of privacy, when it protects that commitment, as drawing a line that precludes state control in a reserved zone of individual privacy. As we'll see, this is one way in which the abortion debate has been framed in American politics.

Second, to live with dignity is to have the wherewithal to live comfortably enough for well-being. Well-being has multiple dimensions: it includes an internal sense of satisfaction and the material conditions in which one lives. It also has a social and participatory aspect, which I have elsewhere referred to as the "dignity of belonging." Some courts have, for instance, insisted that people have the ability to participate on an equal footing in the social and political life of their community. As former South African Constitutional Court Justice Laurie Ackermann has described it, "The notion that 'we are not islands unto ourselves' is central to the understanding of the individual in African thought. It is often expressed in the phrase *umuntu ngumuntu ngabantu* which emphasises 'communality and the inter-dependence of the members of a community' and that every individual is an extension of others."[4] The phrase is usually seen in shorthand as *ubuntu*. Indeed, the harshest forms of punishment (short of death) have always been incarceration, isolation (as in solitary confinement), excommunication, exile, and other forms of cutting a person off from society.

Well-being means at a minimum that people should have access to adequate and clean water, nutritious food, and shelter from the elements. They should have "the highest attainable standard of physical and mental health," as the World Health

Organization says. They should have education to enable them not only to exercise agency over their own lives but also to be able to "mix and intermingle with society."[5] They should be able to have relationships with others and participate in community activities and not be ostracized or marginalized because they have poor health or a disability, or because they are poor or illiterate.

Finally, because we live with others, we need to treat others and be treated by others with dignity. The UDHR itself says in its first article, as it announces the central tenet of dignity, that because we have dignity, we should treat "one another in the spirit of brotherhood." From this, we get the idea of treating someone humanely—as if there is a standard of humanity that cannot be transgressed, a floor below which one should never go. International law, therefore, prohibits in absolute terms certain kinds of treatment, including torture, slavery, genocide, and apartheid, precisely because these are inhumane and therefore can never be justified. People are born with dignity and keep it throughout their lives (and perhaps in some form after death); it is considered inviolable and inalienable as a person can never be separated from their dignity. So every person is always entitled to be treated as a person, no matter what they have done. For this reason, people who have been convicted of even the most heinous crimes retain their dignity rights: we do not torture a person even if they tortured another person.

The Alpha and the Omega

The law of dignity is the foundation of human rights law. It tells us when an injustice has occurred and fuels the fight to protect our own or another person's dignity. But it is also the very purpose of human rights law. We fight for rights, advocate for policies, and go into the streets or into our polling booths because we want a society in which human dignity is respected. We want a future in which our children and the next generations can express themselves more openly, can have more choices and more control over their lives, will live more comfortably, and be treated by all with respect. Dignity is the source of our rights, but it is also the marker of our aspirations.

The idea of human dignity has become the linchpin for how we structure our society, in the United States and throughout the world. It is, as the South African jurist Laurie Ackermann wrote, the "lodestar" of the constitutional system or, as Pakistani Supreme Court Justice Syed Mansoor Ali Shah wrote, "the jewel in the crown of fundamental rights."[6]

But how did we get here? How did the world coalesce around this double helix of an idea that there is something inherently important about each and every human being and that that important something gives us the right to have and to claim rights to give us more freedom, more autonomy, and a better life?

The Phoenix Rising from the Ashes of World War II

We begin at the dawn of the human rights era, before the ashes of World War II had settled on the ground, and when the air was still thick with images of concentration camps, mixed with still-lingering memories of mustard gas and battlefields from just thirty years before. At this moment, delegates from fifty-one nations of the world came together in San Francisco and established the United Nations (UN), whose primary twin goals were "to save succeeding generations from the scourge of war, which twice in our lifetime has brought untold sorrow to mankind," and "to reaffirm faith in fundamental human rights, in the dignity and worth of the human person, in the equal rights of men and women and of nations large and small."[7] With that, the global commitment to human rights was born, with the intuition that faith "in the dignity and worth of the human person" is the foundation of a just society.

In another three years, the UN's Human Rights Commission would submit to the General Assembly for its ratification not an international bill of rights but a Universal Declaration of Human Rights. This document adopts the UN Charter language and reinforces the focus on human dignity. Much has been written about the Commission's reliance on dignity as the basis of human rights, although little is in fact known. There is little "legislative history" about why the term was used as the document's cornerstone, what it meant to the drafters, or how they intended for it to be interpreted. The drafters of the UDHR seemed to choose the word in part because it needed no definition: "the word was embraced and reinterpreted as representing a concept both universally understandable and corresponding to equivalent words or ideas in non-Western cultures."[8]

At the same time, they chose it because of what it did *not* say: in particular, it connoted no particular religion but was consistent with all the major ones. "Committee members from countries representing Hindu, Buddhist, Islamic, and Confucian traditions recognized the term dignity as a reference to the distinctive value or worth of, and the respect owed to, every human being."[9] The idea that this word means more or less the same thing in most languages and cultures certainly makes it a good candidate for inclusion in the UDHR and helps explain its later inclusion in the vast majority of the world's constitutional systems. In every language, the word for dignity translates to some variation on honor, respect, worth, goodness, majesty, importance, or value.[10]

The drafters of the UDHR based the human rights edifice on this idea. And generations of advocates, judges, and drafters around the world have too.

The Inherent Equal Worth of Every Person

It is difficult to overstate the importance that the UDHR assigns to dignity. It is the first concept identified in the Preamble, which opens with this: "Whereas recognition of the inherent dignity and of the equal and inalienable rights of all members of the human family is the foundation of freedom, justice and peace in the world." Later, the Preamble incants the opening words of the UN Charter: "Whereas the peoples of the United Nations have in the Charter reaffirmed their faith in fundamental human rights, in the dignity and worth of the human person and in the equal rights of men and women and have determined to promote social progress and better standards of life in larger freedom." Then, we see dignity again, in the very first article: "All human beings are born free and equal in dignity and rights. They are endowed with reason and conscience and should act towards one another in a spirit of brotherhood."

These phrases have given rise to an understanding of human dignity as denoting the inherent and equal worth of every person. And *that* is a profoundly radical idea. Let's unpack the language in the UDHR. That dignity is inherent means that it is associated with "members of the human family" from birth, just by virtue of being born human. That is, you don't have to earn it like being a duke or a president. It's not based on what you accomplish or who you know. Because it isn't given to you, it can't be taken away. So it's not a right like equality or liberty that governments define and grant or withhold unilaterally on their own terms. Dignity is a quality attached to being human. It just *is*.

That dignity is equal in everyone is necessitated by its inherence. If dignity were not equal, then a person could decide that another has less dignity, and therefore less inherent value. If that's true, the whole house of cards falls down: the logic that one person may have more dignity than another, or that one person may decide who has more or less dignity, leads directly to the logic of the Third Reich, the very ideology the UDHR drafters had as their primary mission to repudiate. They were tasked, after all, with setting the groundwork for a new world order in which ideologies like Nazism could not happen. Since no one can be empowered to make that determination about another person, then all people must have equal human dignity.

And the word "dignity" itself is worth contemplating. The US Supreme Court has talked about the dignity of courtrooms and the dignity of the presidency, but they have also talked about the dignity of rivers, of contracts, of arguments, and more. They seem to use it to denote the importance of something, its gravitas. Along the same lines, Jeremy Waldron has written about dignity as status or rank, associated with royalty and nobles or people of high office.[11] The UDHR does not change that meaning. It just attributes it to every person equally. In response to the old-fashioned sense of dignity as denoting an entitlement to respect that only a few people in a society had, the UDHR says that "every member of the human family" is important and is entitled to respect. Everyone holds the high status of "a person."

A Supremely Radical Idea

This sounds simple and logical. But it's supremely radical. When else in history, where else in the world, have people agreed that every human being is of equal worth? When has the challenge been set down to reject racism, sexism, caste systems, slavery, and discrimination in all its forms? Consider the words of Hernán Santa Cruz of Chile, member of the drafting sub-committee:

> I perceived clearly that I was participating in a truly significant historic event in which a consensus had been reached as to the supreme value of the human person, a value that did not originate in the decision of a worldly power, but rather in the fact of existing—

which gave rise to the inalienable right to live free from want and oppression and to fully develop one's personality. In the Great Hall ... there was an atmosphere of genuine solidarity and brotherhood among men and women from all latitudes, the like of which I have not seen again in any international setting.[12]

In this brief comment, Santa Cruz not only reflects the genuinely momentous spirit of the time but also articulates the basic elements that courts in later generations would seize on to articulate a legal ethic of human dignity.

First, dignity and rights are intertwined: the recognition of human dignity gives rise to human rights or, conversely, rights derive from the fact of human dignity.

Second, dignity has a material component: because people have dignity, they have a right to a life free from want (in the words of Franklin Delano Roosevelt)—that is, to live decently, with dignity.

Third, equal dignity prohibits oppression: it denies to any person the basis for discriminating against, humiliating, or oppressing any other person.

And fourth, dignity is fundamentally about the full development of the human personality. What we all want, the world over, in every culture, in every community, is to be able to fully develop our personhood. Maybe that, ultimately, is what distinguishes human beings from all other living beings. Maybe that's why human dignity matters.

These concepts and even these specific phrases show up over and over throughout the cases. This is the overlapping consensus that is evident from constitutions and judicial decisions around the world.

How Dignity Becomes Law

Dignity starts out as an idea, as the foundational value of the human rights edifice. But it soon becomes a right in and of itself (the right to dignity) or a set of rights (dignity rights) that flow from the legal recognition of human dignity. After its appearance in the UDHR, it becomes the centerpiece of the two International Covenants – one that protects civil and political rights such as voting and expression and conscience and one that protects economic, social, and cultural rights such as education, health, and housing. Unlike the UDHR, these two treaties are binding law on the nations that ratify them, which since the end of the Cold War means almost every nation on earth.[13] Both covenants begin this way:

> The States Parties to the present Covenant,
>
> Considering that, in accordance with the principles proclaimed in the Charter of the United Nations, recognition of the inherent dignity and of the equal and inalienable rights of all members of the human family is the foundation of freedom, justice and peace in the world,
>
> Recognizing that these rights derive from the inherent dignity of the human person,
>
> Recognizing that, in accordance with the Universal Declaration of Human Rights, the ideal of free human beings enjoying freedom from fear and want can only be achieved if conditions are created whereby everyone may enjoy his [economic, social and cultural rights, and his civil and political rights].

The remaining sections of these covenants list the rights to which ratifying countries are bound to guarantee. But by sourcing all those rights in "the inherent dignity and of the equal and inalienable rights of all members of the human family," it becomes clear that every human right flows from there.

Once countries are bound by international law to protect the rights listed in the International Covenants, it is not a great leap to put them in their constitutions: the commitment is already accepted, and the language is already there.

Here are some examples of what dignity language looks like in constitutions:

Dignity as a foundational value:

Spain: "The dignity of the person, the inviolable rights which are inherent, the free development of the personality, the respect for the law and for the rights of others are the foundation of political order and social peace."

Peru: "The defense of the human person and respect for his dignity are the supreme purpose of the society and the State."

Dignity as a fundamental right:

Germany: "Human dignity shall be inviolable. To respect and protect it shall be the duty of all state authority."

Belgium: "Everyone has the right to lead a life in keeping with human dignity."

New Zealand Bill of Rights Act: "Everyone deprived of liberty shall be treated with humanity and with respect for the inherent dignity of the person."

South Africa: "Everyone has inherent dignity and the right to have their dignity respected and protected."

Ukraine: "Everyone has the right to respect of his or her dignity. No one shall be subjected to torture, cruel, inhuman or degrading treatment or punishment that violates his or her dignity."

Dignity and equality:

Mexico: "Any form of discrimination, based on ethnic or national origin, gender, age, disabilities, social status, medical conditions, religion, opinions, sexual orientation, marital status, or any other form, which violates the human dignity or seeks to annul or diminish the rights and freedoms of the people, is prohibited."

Taiwan (Republic of China): "The State shall protect the dignity of women, safeguard their personal safety, eliminate sexual discrimination, and further substantive gender equality."

Italy: "All citizens have equal social dignity and are equal before the law, without distinction of sex, race, language, religion, political opinion, personal and social conditions."

Dignity and private life:

Japan: "With regard to choice of spouse, property rights, inheritance, choice of domicile, divorce and other matters pertaining to marriage and the family, laws shall be enacted from the standpoint of individual dignity and the essential equality of the sexes."

Pakistan: "The dignity of man and, subject to law, the privacy of home, shall be inviolable."

Dignity for especially vulnerable people:

Tunisia: "Every prisoner shall have the right to humane treatment that preserves their dignity." "Children are guaranteed the rights to dignity, health, care and education from their parents and the state."

Algeria: "The living conditions of citizens below the legal working age and those who cannot work or can never work again shall be guaranteed by the State within a framework of respect for human dignity."

Finland: "No one shall be sentenced to death, tortured or otherwise treated in a manner violating human dignity." "Those who cannot obtain the means necessary for a life of dignity have the right to receive indispensable subsistence and care."

And so on. We see dignity in more than six hundred provisions in more than 170 constitutions (out of about 194 countries in the world).

The pivot from international law to constitutional law is critical. There are many differences between legal obligations at the international level and in the domestic sphere of constitutional law, but the principal one is this: constitutional law is enforced in countries with constitutional courts. At the international level, it's nearly impossible for a person to get a judgment against a country to remedy the violation of their rights and to have that judgment enforced. But when there is a court with jurisdiction to review the constitutionality of a government law or act (such as all of our federal courts), then it's much more routine for a court to rule that the government has violated a person's rights and order a remedy. Thus, if dignity had remained only a mainstay of international law, we would not have much to say about it; the fact that it is now recognized in almost every constitution on earth and that courts are interpreting and applying those clauses gives them life. Among the most active constitutional courts in developing a body of dignity law are those in Brazil, Canada, Colombia, Germany, India, Kenya, Malawi, Mexico, Nepal, Pakistan, Peru, South Africa, and Taiwan. In addition, the regional human rights systems in Europe, the Americas, and Africa have been strongly committed to dignity rights throughout their jurisprudence for many years. And they have done so in broad and expansive ways, in cases involving matters as diverse as pensions, housing, voting, education, immigration, gender identity, and more. Many other countries, such as the United States, have a few court decisions that center on or invoke human dignity, even if it is not (yet) a prominent part of their body of constitutional law.

Here are some examples of how courts have been talking about human dignity in the last few years alone.[14]

> India (2022), about the right to abortion: The right to dignity encapsulates the right of every individual to be treated as a self-governing entity having intrinsic value. It means that every human being possesses dignity merely by being a human, and can make self-defining and self-determining choices. Dignity forms a part of the basic structure of the Constitution. Such is its fundamental value in our legal system—the concept of dignity forms the very foundation to the Constitution and the rights enshrined in it. Dignity inheres in every individual and is an inalienable aspect of one's humanity.[15]

> South Africa (2022), about rape: [Every] moment that the applicant was subjected to the violent assault, represents a moment in which her dignity, autonomy and personal security were stripped away. These are values that go to the heart of the human condition. Each rape, for as long as it continues, is an individual affront on a person's dignity.[16]

> European Court of Human Rights (2020), about the need to investigate and prosecute hate crimes: [It] may well suffice that the victim is humiliated in his or her own eyes, even if not in the eyes of others. Indeed, it has previously been established that, although a person does not undergo serious physical or mental suffering, an assault on his or her dignity and physical integrity may constitute degrading treatment.[17]

> Racial violence is a particular affront to human dignity and, in view of its perilous consequences, requires from the authorities special vigilance and a vigorous reaction. It is for this reason that the authorities must use all available means to combat racism and racist violence, thereby reinforcing democracy's vision of a society in which diversity is not perceived as a threat but as a source of enrichment.[18]

> Pakistan (2022), about discrimination against people with disabilities: Therefore, the minimum right to dignity of the minorities and

persons with disabilities is that they ought to be considered equally with the rest of the [rights] of persons with fuller abilities.[19]

Canada (2022), about excessively long prison sentences: Although dignity is not recognized as an independent constitutional right, it is a fundamental value that serves as a guide for the interpretation of all Charter rights. Generally speaking, the concept of dignity evokes the idea that every person has intrinsic worth and is therefore entitled to respect. This respect is owed to every individual, irrespective of their actions.[20]

Malawi (2023), invalidating vagrancy laws: To presume that a person is guilty because he or she appears to be without means is a violation of a person's right to dignity.[21]

United States, 5th Circuit (2023), invalidating voter suppression law: The protections to individual liberty and dignity afforded by each provision of the Constitution do not evaporate when one provision permits states to legislate in a certain field.[22]

United States, D. Del. (2023), about the rights of prisoners to be treated humanely: Dignity, or respect of our fellow human beings, is an important principle underlying many constitutional rights. Because of this, the Supreme Court has routinely discussed dignity in cases where plaintiffs seek to vindicate those rights. . . . Although these claims for violating dignity are not independently recognized, Plaintiffs may proceed with other claims, such as those for Eighth and Fourteenth Amendment violations, that seek to remedy the same underlying violations of their dignity.[23]

In these cases, judges are using their power not only to decide cases but also to explain and develop the idea of human dignity. But this isn't just a philosophical exercise: these are constitutional cases—cases in which judges are holding the government to account for violating human dignity and insisting that the government, by act or omission, ensure the protection of each person's dignity. These cases matter to people. This is how dignity gets written into law.

Collectively, these cases show how dignity rights protect every human being and touch nearly every aspect of the human experience. And sometimes we can see how dignity becomes law that changes things, how it transforms the law, and by extension, can help transform a nation. In South Africa, the Constitutional Court relied on the right to dignity to find that the death penalty was unconstitutional. In Europe, the European Court of Human Rights criminalized marital rape because it violates the dignity of married women. In Canada, South Africa, the United States, Mexico, and elsewhere, courts have held that laws prohibiting same-sex marriage are unconstitutional because they violate the dignity rights of people who want to marry; and in Nepal, India, and elsewhere, courts have held that restricting people to binary gender identification violates the dignity of people who identify as neither male nor female but as a third gender. In Colombia, Nepal, and elsewhere, courts are recognizing the rights of nature and the right to live in harmony with a healthy and sustainable ecology because no one can live with dignity in a polluted environment. In all these cases (and others), dignity is not only defining the outer boundaries of the law; it is pushing those boundaries forward, helping transform societies in humanistic ways. This book considers how we might do that in the United States.

The Language of Dignity

For our purposes, considering dignity in the United States, these cases may be most important for another reason. Dignity is not an incantation; it's a set of ideas that, together, show what it means to be human in the twenty-first century and what important human values the law needs to protect. This vocabulary of dignity that courts have developed, in the United States and abroad, can be organized into three baskets of rights, or according to three principles that, collectively, cover almost all the uses of dignity in the global case law. These can be articulated in any order.

First, dignity represents the inherent and equal worth of every human being. Because each person has worth as a function of being born a member of the human family, each person's life matters. For many courts, this entitles each person to the right to fully and freely develop as a person and to define for themselves their unique identity. It guarantees the right to have control over one's life or life project. We repeatedly see phrases like "the free development of the personality," to be treated "as a person," to "be considered equally" with others in society, "self-defining" and "self-determining," autonomy and agency, and the avoidance of objectification, humiliation, degradation, and inhuman treatment. It prohibits discrimination that limits the fullness of one's personality—treatment that considers a person not in terms of the person's individual qualities but as part of a group or with a presumed set of characteristics or traits. This set of rights also includes the right to freedom of expression, freedom of conscience, and political rights to participate in democratic activity, as well as rights relating to gender and sexual identity. In some constitutional cultures, these rights also include the right to psychological integrity, including the right to retain hope and the right to not have one's personality altered. This can be thought of as the principle of personhood because it protects what is most essential and unique to each individual and protects the right to develop and grow throughout one's life. For obvious reasons, we should be especially careful when the dignity of children and youth is at risk.

Second, courts talk about the right to be treated with dignity. They use words relating to bodily integrity, freedom from humiliation, and protection from vulnerability. We can think of this as a principle of humanity because it implies that there are certain things that human beings simply cannot do to other humans. This aspect of dignity protects against man's inhumanity to man. It includes the absolute ban on torture, inhumane conditions of custody and incarceration, and all forms of humiliating and degrading treatment. Sometimes, it protects a person's privacy, securing for each person that realm that is truly and uniquely theirs. Using the UDHR language, some cases describe this as the right to be treated "as a person," as if human personhood mandates its own inherent standard of behavior.

Third, the right to live with dignity relates to material and social goods, including not only the fulfillment of biological necessities for life such as food, water, health care, and a healthy environment but also education and cultural assets. Most of these interests are not guaranteed under the US Constitution for anyone, but they describe what it means to live with dignity. This can be thought of as the principle of decency because it entails a quality of life that is at least decent. Some courts refer to this as a right to a dignified life or a dignified standard of living (*vida digna*). For courts in many countries, it includes the ability to interact in society with others, to fully participate in society on an equal basis with others, and to belong to a community. This has both political and social dimensions because poverty functions as an excluder and separator.

Collectively, the recognition of these rights is the foundation of a just society. Indeed, the American Bar Association has affirmed that "human dignity—the inherent, equal, and inalienable worth of every person—is foundational to a just rule of law" and that "'dignity rights'—the principle that human dignity is fundamental to all areas of law and policy—[should] be reflected in the exercise of [all] legislative, executive, and judicial functions."[24]

This commitment to human dignity as a central pillar of the law—the very foundation of a "just" rule of law—and buttressed by the thousands of cases throughout the world, seems to me persuasive evidence that dignity is an important and useful concept in resolving social and legal issues. Most books about dignity in law begin with defensive responses to the claims by some that dignity is too broad, too elastic, too amorphous, too subjective, or too something else to be useful. This book skips that counterargument mainly because courts and tribunals around the world skip it and go straight to using it to resolve claims, thus negating the argument that it isn't useful. In the process, they have developed a vocabulary, and a perspective of the most fundamental values of humanity that is clear, precise, and well defined. We will use this language throughout this book to show how policies can be tailored to respect, protect, and promote human dignity in these ways in the United States.

Some Perplexities

Of course, it's not always that easy. While dignity stands for a simple and elegant ideal of full personhood free from want and oppression, there are some hidden questions that continue to perplex. Here are a few; others will appear in the following pages as we consider dignity in the context of specific social issues.

Who Has Dignity?

First, to whom does dignity attach? The UDHR answers that clearly: to everyone born a human being, and only to human beings. Human beings have human rights because they have human dignity. As Article 1 explains, humans are different because "they are endowed with reason and conscience." But of course this is not equally true for all humans at all times. Newborns have little capacity for reason, and some adults make terribly wrongheaded decisions, while others are geniuses. And there are as many saints as there are sinners. If reason and conscience are not distributed evenly across the human population, then why is dignity? The UDHR does not explain; it merely asserts that it is so, regardless. That is, to enjoy the benefits of human dignity, it is enough to be born a member of a family that, overall, is endowed with reason and conscience.

Although the UDHR is concerned only with humans, it expresses no opinion on the possible dignity claims of nonhumans that are inanimate and man-made, such as corporations or states, courts, or contracts. All of these may be accorded dignity, but not the human dignity with which the UDHR is concerned. Nor does it attach to natural entities such as rivers or dolphins or ecosystems, such as are implicated in the recent rights-of-nature movement that has taken hold in some Latin American countries and elsewhere.[25] The UDHR, as well as the human rights movement that has grown out of it and therefore this book, makes no judgment about the dignity claims of nonhumans. It simply asserts the dignity rights of humans.

The drafters made another crucial decision: dignity attaches to the individual human person, to each individual member of the human family. It does not attach to groups or communities or cultures or nations. Even though these may be important to identity, human flourishing, and development, they are important precisely because they contribute to the full development of each person's individual worth, not because they are independent of it. Again, the logic of the Holocaust provided the counterexample: if an idea or a group or a nation can claim dignity, then it can demand a sacrifice of the human person in the name of that dignity. To refute that possibility, the drafters insisted that the human dignity of each individual person is preeminent.

There may be another reason for the attachment of dignity to humans and not corporations or states or ideologies. Although many of the drafters were influenced by different philosophical and religious conceptions of dignity, one of the primary sources for the modern conception of human dignity is what has become

known as the anti-objectification principle, most often associated with the eighteenth-century German philosopher Im-
manuel Kant. Kant's central insight on the question of human
dignity was simply that a person should be treated as an end in
and of himself or herself, not as a means or object to accomplish
another person's ends. This is why rape, slavery, and other forms
of abuse violate the principle of human dignity: one person uses
another to achieve their own ends. It may also help explain why
dignity attaches to humans (and other natural beings) but not to
things that people have created or invented. Nonnatural beings
(such as corporations or states or a political party) have purposes
by which their value can be measured; natural beings simply
exist, so their value cannot be measured or qualified. It is simply
accepted and recognized for what it is.

Is There Enough Dignity for Everyone?

In 2013 and 2015, the Supreme Court ruled in a pair of 5–4 decisions that same-sex couples had equal rights as opposite-sex
couples to marry. These holdings are in line with decisions from
courts in South Africa, Brazil, Canada, Taiwan, India, and
Mexico and in much of the European Union and Latin America,
many of which have relied on human dignity. In the first case,
the Court ruled that the federal Defense of Marriage Act, which
prohibited recognition of same-sex marriages at the federal level
(i.e., for tax and other purposes) was unconstitutional because it
had no legitimate purpose or effect other than to "disparage and
to injure those whom the State, by its marriage laws, sought to
protect in personhood and dignity. By seeking to displace this
protection and treating those persons as living in marriages less
respected than others, the federal statute is in violation of the
Fifth Amendment."[26] This is the only mention of dignity in the
case that aligns with the global cases about same-sex relations.

Elsewhere, the Court uses "dignity" in the sense of status or as an abstraction, conferring it on the relationship but not the people within the relationship. But here, the Court associates it with personhood, suggesting that decisions about marriage go to the core of who we are as people and how we choose to live our lives. And *that* goes to human dignity.

In the second decision, *Obergefell v. Hodges*, Justice Anthony Kennedy started to find his footing in dignity and, locating the right to same-sex marriage at the confluence of equal protection and due process rights, found:

> The fundamental liberties protected by the Fourteenth Amendment extend to certain personal choices central to individual dignity and autonomy, including intimate choices defining personal identity and beliefs.[27]

This gets us much closer to the ways dignity is used in the global case law and in this book. Marriage, he says, is associated with the core values that make a person who they are, and the state cannot limit those choices. Now, whether or not we agree that marriage is as sacred and noble as Justice Kennedy asserted, the underlying point is the critical one: neither the state nor the federal government has the power to limit those aspects of a person that are central to their core identity and that go to the most intimate choices we make about how we live our lives. This is not as much a matter of autonomy—that is, the ability to make one's own rules—as identity.

This is what Justice John Roberts does not get when he laments in his *Obergefell* dissent that

> the majority's reasoning would apply with equal force to the claim of a fundamental right to plural marriage. If "there is dignity in the bond between two men or two women who seek to marry and in their autonomy to make such profound choices," why would there be any less dignity in the bond between three people who, in exercising their autonomy, seek to make the profound choice to marry?[28]

But for the vast majority of people, there is a difference between choosing to marry a person of the same sex and choosing
to marry more than one other person; the first is a matter of a
person's core identity and personhood, while the second is extremely unlikely to be so. If dignity were only about autonomy,
then a person could make a dignity claim about anything: I want
to make my own rules about cigarette smoking or not going to
work on Fridays or shooting my neighbor's dog because it barks
all night. But governments do have the power to limit some
choices people make; that's exactly what the regulatory power of
government is. But the point of cases like *Obergefell* is that while
the government can limit what you do, it can't limit who you are.
And that is the point of the dignity lens.

This is why the argument for discrimination is not a meaningful counterargument to the claim for equality. Even when the
former is cloaked in religious garb or in free-speech rights, the
choice to discriminate—whether it manifests as the choice not
to provide services for same-sex couples, as in some recent Supreme Court cases, or the decision to engage in racist speech or
conduct—does not typically go to a person's core identity. It is the
rare person who can say that the need to discriminate against
others is core to their identity and their "authorship" over their
life as the decision of whom to marry and whether to have children. These are not equivalent. Equality protects core identity
values; discrimination permits certain actions.[29]

And this is why dignity is not a zero-sum game. There is
enough dignity to go around for everyone. In the case of same-
sex marriage, expanding dignity rights to allow everyone to
marry the person they love does not take away from the dignity
of those who do not support same-sex marriage; they still have
their dignity in their heterosexual identity and in their opposite-
sex marriages. The restriction on discrimination is like restrictions on other behaviors that society seeks to control for one

reason or another; it limits their actions but does not reach who they are as people.

And this is why promoting dignity is a goal that everyone should be able to agree on. Everyone wins.

If Dignity Is an Inherent Human Trait, What Has Law Got to Do with It?

If dignity is so central to a person's core identity that it's intrinsic to who we are, why do we need laws to protect it? Isn't dignity there, no matter what? Well, yes—and no. Here we have to distinguish between an inherent aspect of the human condition and the law's response to that inherent quality. Justice Clarence Thomas addressed the problem directly in his dissent in *Obergefell v. Hodges.* He began by accepting the importance and the innateness of human dignity, which he associated with the Christian principle of *imago dei.* But he rejected the argument that dignity gives rise to constitutional rights:

> Human dignity has long been understood in this country to be innate. When the Framers proclaimed in the Declaration of Independence that "all men are created equal" and "endowed by their Creator with certain unalienable Rights," they referred to a vision of mankind in which all humans are created in the image of God and therefore of inherent worth. That vision is the foundation upon which this Nation was built.
>
> The corollary of that principle is that human dignity cannot be taken away by the government. Slaves did not lose their dignity (any more than they lost their humanity) because the government allowed them to be enslaved. Those held in internment camps did not lose their dignity because the government confined them. And those denied governmental benefits certainly do not lose their dignity because the government denies them those benefits. The government cannot bestow dignity, and it cannot take it away.[30]

In his view, the law cannot touch our innate human dignity, and it is therefore irrelevant to the protection of dignity. Thomas chides the *Obergefell* majority for demeaning those who believe that allowing some couples to marry degrades the institution of marriage. The majority's "musings," he says, "can have no effect on the dignity of the persons the majority demeans"—that is, those who maintain a "traditional" view of marriage and those who believe that "one's liberty, not to mention one's dignity, was something to be shielded from—not provided by—the State." The issues here are complex and raise two interrelated sets of questions.

First, Justice Thomas's central challenge is that if dignity is innate and inheres in each person no matter what, then what difference does it make what the law does? But it *does* matter, very much. It is true that the government does not grant and cannot withhold human dignity. But it is also true—and this is the point that Thomas misses—that it can support it, protect it, and help fulfill its promise. The law can be shaped to protect people from want by ensuring an adequate and accessible supply of nutritious food, it can shield people from humiliation and protect their vulnerabilities by punishing those who would discriminate and oppress, and it can provide free education to all at high standards to ensure that everyone can fully develop and flourish. Or the law can make other decisions and increase want, allow or even require oppression, and increase stress and anxiety by making health care expensive and inefficacious. Laws affect how we live. A parent worries about whether to buy food or pay rent because minimum pay is too low and subsidies for families have been cut. A man lies alone in his cell looking at the ceiling day after day because he has been given a life sentence for crime he may not have committed. A child languishes in school because the music and arts programs have been cut. Dignity still beats in the heart, but the struggle to live with dignity gnaws at the soul. The global jurisprudence of dignity rights—that body of law from around the world in which courts have protected human dignity claims against governments—proves that law *is* relevant to the experience of human dignity. As the Supreme Court of India explained, "Although human dignity inheres in every individual, it is susceptible to violation by external conditions and treatment imposed by the state."[31] The law matters to dignity, and dignity should matter to the law.

So this leads to the second question that Justice Thomas raises: If the state can choose to enhance or diminish dignity, if it can protect it or "dent" it (as one Indian court has said), then we must ask what kind of legal system we want. Here Justice Thomas again posits an answer that is plausible, but not really satisfying. For Justice Thomas, dignity is best protected by shielding people from the state. If this is true in America, it's out of line with the expectations of most people in most countries around the world, where government is expected to provide education and health care at least to the best of its available resources. But it may not even be true for most people in America who also want those things and expect government to do more to help support their life of dignity than simply to stay out of the way.

So both can be true: dignity is innate and the law can protect it or threaten it. So what should the law do? What should our public policies do?

If Everyone Has Dignity, Why Doesn't Everyone Live with Dignity?

The last conundrum we address here has to do with how we use dignity in society and in our laws. How do we reconcile the *is* and the *ought*: the beautiful affirmation that every person has inherent dignity with the ugly reality that hundreds of millions of people, or nearly 10 percent of the world's population, live in *extreme* poverty;[32] that people are being slaughtered in warfare every day; and that slavery, including child slavery, and human trafficking still exist? People who live in such conditions are not free from want or oppression, and they are not able to freely develop their personalities, to live their lives on their own terms, and to flourish. They surely have inherent and inalienable human dignity, but the conditions of the world have made it impossible for them to live with dignity.

So we need to focus on the conditions of the world, and how those conditions came to be, and why, and, most important for our purposes, what can be done to minimize the dignity-diminishing effects of social conditions. What kinds of laws and policies should we have in this country to enhance the ability of more people to live their fullest lives?

We can approach the problem from either direction. We can start with the question of policies and ask what kinds of policies we want that will enhance human dignity. Or we can start with the divisions in the country around certain policies and ask how we can resolve those in ways that unify rather than divide and that enhance and protect dignity rather than leave it vulnerable. Either way, we have to ask: Can the turn toward dignity help us resolve our most pressing social issues?

TWO

Dignity as the Touchstone of Racial Justice

The "Wicked Problems" of Race, Racism, and Affirmative Action

Racial justice in twenty-first-century America is what might be called a "wicked problem." Problems are wicked not because they are bad or evil but because they are particularly resistant to resolution. The causes and effects of racial justice is far beyond the scope of this book to examine seriously, but it's enough to see that it's a wicked problem because its resolution depends on so many unknown variables: some of the biggest fault lines include whether we understand race as merely a social construct or as a biological fact or social fact; whether the prevalent injustices in America today are primarily functions of race or primarily functions of other socioeconomic disparities; how to think about affirmative action and reparations and whether they are necessary or misguided; and whether racial justice itself is the remedy for the racial disparities that pervade American society and the widening gaps we see between communities that are predominantly white and those that are predominantly black or brown.

To name just a few. We aim for racial justice, but we don't really know how to get there or what it would look like. And we should consider the possibility that broader-based policies aimed at social justice could be as effective in alleviating the harms of racism as policies focused more specifically on remedying past racial harms. But it depends on myriad factors. These are all wickedly complicated questions.

The Supreme Court has not helped the matter. Rather than carefully tackle the nuances, sensitivities, and subtle distinctions that make these problems so wicked, the Supreme Court in June 2023 took a sledgehammer to the issue and ended all consideration of race as a factor in decision-making in public and most private universities and, by extension, in most public and many private institutions of all kinds. The holding in *Students for Fair Admissions* (an Orwellian name) *v. Harvard* and *Students for Fair Admissions v. University of North Carolina* could extend to decisions about hiring and granting benefits across the federal government and to all state and private agencies that receive federal funds:[1] from now on, virtually all of these can be held liable for considering race as a factor in any decision.[2]

Let's start with how the Court sees the problem, and the solution, and then we will look at this through the lens of human dignity. From the Court's perspective, government used race as a basis for "sorting" people (to use Justice Thomas's peculiar word) under slavery (1619–1863) and during Jim Crow (1877–1960s). After the Civil War, the Constitution was amended by a trio of "Reconstruction Amendments," the centerpiece of which is the guarantee in the Fourteenth Amendment (1868) that "no state shall . . . deny to any person within its jurisdiction the equal protection of the laws." The Court reads this mandate as a compelled rule of "color-blindness"—a phrase drawn from Justice John Marshall Harlan's lone dissent in *Plessy v. Ferguson* (the 1896 case that, over his dissent, inaugurated the Jim Crow era of profound racial exclusion and segregation). Justice Harlan wrote: "There is no caste here. Our Constitution is color-blind, and neither knows nor tolerates classes among citizens."[3] For the modern Court, these four words—"Our Constitution is color-blind"—is all you need to answer any problem related to race in America. Who should get admitted to university, who should be offered jobs, what kinds of companies should get government contracts or awards or benefits: let administrators do their job, but as to race, they must be absolutely color-blind. This is such a hard rule that race may not even be used "as a factor" among many others in the decision-making process.[4]

This is wrongheaded for so many reasons, it's hard to know where to begin. Let's just mention a few. For starters, it disingenuously cleanses an ugly history. The Court's account of America's racial history is so woefully inadequate that it reduces centuries of slavery and Jim Crow to a sorting problem, as if a Harry Potter hat had gone wonky; it entirely fails to recognize our racist history as a form of barbarous violence against human beings that was written into law and scarred into bodies over generations, and leaving legacies of inequity and inequality that persist to this day. Then, revealing its utter moral and intellectual bankruptcy, the Court finds a lamentably jejune solution—just stop sorting! This "remedy" to racial discrimination written in 1896 by a man who had owned black slaves and did not free them until he was forced to by a constitutional amendment. Can we not find a more suitable moral leader to guide us through this wicked morass in the twenty-first century? Have we not learned anything about race in America in the 130 years since that sentence was written?

The Court's account of the present gives no more confidence. It ignores the current reality of race in America today, where discrepancies in health, wealth, income, criminal law, literacy rates, mortality rates, and more are all racially delineated.

This is not just a narrative problem. By ignoring the real

harms of past oppression and present-day injustices, the Court entirely fails to distinguish between "sorting" for the purpose of denigration and "sorting" for the purpose of equity and inclusion. It reckons with the past only by ignoring its harms. The Court has long suggested that there is no constitutional distinction between apartheid and affirmative action, but this completely denies the insult to human dignity that undergirds the first and is assuaged by the second. The reason for this is simple to see, though unstated. For the Court, in any "sorting" process, there are winners and losers and any benefit to one person is a burden to another. A seat that goes to one person is taken away from another and if the basis for giving the seat to a person is race, then the reason for taking it away from someone else is because of race, and that is unconstitutional. The Court sees a dog-eat-dog world of scarce resources and nefariously motivated bureaucrats, where any benefit is not so much a public good but a zero-sum game.

Despite all that is historically wrong, factually distorted, and racially insensitive in the Court's opinion, it does contain one valuable nugget of insight: sorting people by category is wrong because it fails to treat each person "as a person"—as an individual human being, with their own story and experiences, and their own unique personhood. If we start with this insight, we can build a dignity-based approach to affirmative action and social justice.

The Court's Affirmative Action

According to its website, Students for Fair Admissions (SFFA)

is a nonprofit membership group of more than 20,000 students, parents, and others who believe that racial classifications and pref-

erences in college admissions are unfair, unnecessary, and unconstitutional. Our mission is to support and participate in litigation
that will restore the original principles of our nation's civil rights
movement: A student's race and ethnicity should not be factors
that either harm or help that student to gain admission to a com-
petitive university.[5]

SFFA challenged the admissions processes at both Harvard
University (a private university) and University of North Carolina (a public university); both receive federal funds and are
therefore subject to federal constitutional controls. SFFA made
its case to the US Supreme Court, and the Court agreed.

As the *SFFA* Court explains, the problem with using race as a
factor in decision-making "is well established."

Outright racial balancing [is] "patently unconstitutional." That is
so, we have repeatedly explained, because "at the heart of the Constitution's guarantee of equal protection lies the simple command
that the Government must treat citizens as individuals, not as
simply components of a racial, religious, sexual or national class.[6]

The very last paragraph of Chief Justice John Roberts's opinion provides a few examples of how admissions decisions may
be made, without using race as a factor but based on each applicant's "own merit and essential qualities." It is worth quoting at
length:

At the same time . . . nothing in this opinion should be construed as
prohibiting universities from considering an applicant's discussion
of how race affected his or her life, be it through discrimination,
inspiration, or otherwise. . . . A benefit to a student who overcame
racial discrimination, for example, must be tied to *that student's*
courage and determination. Or a benefit to a student whose heritage or culture motivated him or her to assume a leadership role or
attain a particular goal must be tied to *that student's* unique ability
to contribute to the university. In other words, the student must
be treated based on his or her experiences as an individual—not
on the basis of race. Many universities have for too long done just

the opposite. And in doing so, they have concluded, wrongly, that
the touchstone of an individual's identity is not challenges bested,
skills built, or lessons learned but the color of their skin. Our constitutional history does not tolerate that choice.[7]

Whether or not this was the Court's intent, this passage lays
out the basis of a dignity-based way to promote social justice and
even racial justice, by allowing each person to be judged based
not on government-created categories but on their own telling
of their own story. This is, of course, what Dr. Martin Luther
King meant when he dreamed of a day when all people would be
judged "not by the color of their skin but by the content of their
character." The Court's approach does not prohibit any applicant
from telling their story in their own way, according to their own
perspective and experiences, including their story of their own
experience of race. In fact, it encourages it. It removes race as an
abstract category and converts it to a lived experience. It therefore advances each person's dignity by ensuring that each person
owns their story and can tell it as they want to.

This approach also advances a broader dignity of social
justice. Focusing on how applicants or candidates for jobs or
bidders for government contracts have overcome adversity (including racial adversity) or think about their racial identity in
connection with other aspects of their identity may advance diversity in the classroom, inclusion in the workplace, and equity
in the allocation of government benefits. For one thing, it may
help avoid the problem of objectification: universities that admit
applicants of color to have a critical mass of nonwhite students
in the classroom to provide balance and ensure diversity can be
said to be objectifying the students by using them (admittedly
for their own benefit) to accomplish the university's goals. In
addition, the reliance on categories tends to obscure differences
and diversities within those categories. The *SFFA* approach
could also promote social justice and, by implication, racial

justice without overdetermining the meaning of race itself. It could avoid some of the most wicked features of racial injustice in America by allowing people to express their racial experience in their own terms. This may be a more direct way of getting to the broader goal: a society in which more people can live with more dignity.

Using this individualized, applicant-centered approach as our point of departure, we can now start to build a framework based on dignity consciousness to advance racial and social justice.

A Dignity-Based Approach to Social Justice

Rejecting race consciousness in favor of dignity consciousness invites us to think more broadly about why dignity is important to people. Dignity consciousness suggests at least three ways in which the law can improve people's lives: dignity consciousness promotes the right to the full and free development of the human personality; dignity ensures the right to equality however that is achieved, including affirmative action; and dignity claims the right to individualized treatment. These are interconnected rights because people experience their dignity and the threats to their dignity not as independent rights silos but as fluidly interdependent and indivisible. And they are all connected to education.

Dignity and Education

Seventy years ago, the US Supreme Court issued its most important decision ever on the importance of education in America. In the famous case of *Brown v. Board of Education*, a unanimous Court wrote:

Today, education is perhaps the most important function of state and local governments. Compulsory school attendance laws and the great expenditures for education both demonstrate our recognition of the importance of education to our democratic society. It is required in the performance of our most basic public responsibilities, even service in the armed forces. It is the very foundation of good citizenship. Today it is a principal instrument in awakening the child to cultural values, in preparing him for later professional training, and in helping him to adjust normally to his environment. In these days, it is doubtful that any child may reasonably be expected to succeed in life if he is denied the opportunity of an education. Such an opportunity, where the state has undertaken to provide it, is a right which must be made available to all on equal terms.[8]

It is rather surprising that there are so few Supreme Court decisions about education, and none that go beyond *Brown* in reinforcing its importance. In fact, the Court has never recognized a right to education based in the US Constitution or a right to fair funding of education.[9] As even this opinion makes clear ("where the state has undertaken to provide it"), the states are not federally obligated to provide education for anyone. Rather, the Court has recognized the privacy right of parents to make decisions about their children's education,[10] and, incredibly, it has even recognized a religious-based right of parents to deny their children the right to education once they are fifteen.[11] More broadly privileging religious rights over public education, the Court has in a series of cases protected the rights of parents who can afford it to use state funds to avoid public schools altogether in favor of private and religious education for their children, thereby depleting the resources of the public school systems.[12]

But the Court has never protected the right to a decent education as a matter of national law. It is not surprising that the federal Constitution—written at a time when public education was not common, free, universal, or compulsory[13]—does not guarantee education as an obligation of the federal government.

But it is surprising that, in the 235 years since the Constitution was adopted, the Supreme Court has never deemed public education of sufficient importance to read it into the Constitution as a matter of fundamental liberty, either to ensure that every person can freely and fully develop their personality or to contribute to each person's ability to live a life of dignity in community with others.

The international community sees it differently. Article 26 of the UDHR makes this clear: "Education shall be directed to the full development of the human personality."[14]

The Indian Supreme Court has written extensively about this. In a landmark case finding that the right to life in the Constitution includes the right to live with dignity and the right to dignity includes the right to education, the Court wrote: "It is primarily education which brings forth the dignity of a man." Noting the problem of illiteracy throughout India, the Court insisted on accessible education for all because "an individual cannot be assured of human dignity unless his personality is developed and the only way to do that is to educate him. . . . [Other rights] cannot be appreciated and fully enjoyed unless a citizen is educated and is conscious of his individualistic dignity."[15] This echoes, but goes far beyond, the sentiments expressed in *Brown*.

Likewise, the Supreme Federal Tribunal in Brazil has explained:

> The guarantee of comprehensive education must be seen as a necessary means, indispensable for access or, at least, for the most effective possibility of access to the fruits of social and economic development, and therefore, the acquisition of a socio-cultural condition that promotes, in concrete terms, the great ideal of the dignity of the human person and the realization of each one's life project.[16]

For many people in all parts of the world, the link between education and the fulfillment of dignity is crystal clear.

As a practical matter, the lack of protection for public education in the federal constitutional system is, however, alleviated by the language in all fifty state constitutions that "mandates the creation of a public education system."[17] It is guaranteed in each state, but it is not part of our national identity or our value system as Americans.

As a result, education in the United States is lackluster compared to education in our peer countries,[18] and it is racially inequitable. The problem largely comes down to how we fund education, which is both inadequate and unequal.

> The U.S. educational system is one of the most unequal in the industrialized world, and . . . students routinely receive dramatically different learning opportunities based on their social status. In contrast to European and Asian nations that fund schools centrally and equally, the wealthiest 10% of school districts in the United States spend nearly 10 times more than the poorest 10%, and spending ratios of 3 to 1 are common within states. Poor and minority students are concentrated in the least well-funded schools, most of which are located in central cities or rural areas and funded at levels substantially below those of neighboring suburban districts.
>
> Not only do funding systems allocate fewer resources to poor urban districts than to their suburban neighbors, but studies consistently show that, *within* these districts, schools with high concentrations of low-income and "minority" students receive fewer instructional resources than others in the same district. And tracking systems exacerbate these inequalities by segregating many low-income and minority students within schools.[19]

The consequences of these policies are exactly what one would expect: "In combination, policies associated with school funding, resource allocations, and tracking leave minority students with fewer and lower-quality books, curriculum materials, laboratories, and computers; significantly larger class sizes; less qualified and experienced teachers; and less access to high-quality curriculum."[20] In fact, the consequences are so predictable it is hard to avoid the conclusion that they are intended.

> The nation continues to see the effect of systemic and structural barriers to opportunity for Black, Latinx, Native American, and some Asian American and Pacific Islander children, not to mention the ongoing segregation and isolation of students from families with low incomes who are locked into under-resourced schools. . . . Moreover, Americans with higher levels of education are more likely to vote, to volunteer, and to donate to charity.[21]

This is surely a problem of racism and of the country's racist past, but it is also a problem of vast inequalities of wealth spread throughout the country. Poverty and hunger and education deserts are not problems because of slavery or even Jim Crow; they are the result of policies and laws that are in place now. These matters are discussed in more detail in Chapter 6.

A dignity-based approach to educational opportunities would address the importance of education to foster the full and free development of each person's personality; as a public and necessary good in a democracy; as a social and economic equalizer; and as a conduit to social, cultural, and political engagement. A judicial commitment to dignity would protect and promote the right of every person to a quality education. These values apply to all levels of education, including university.

Despite its failings, the Supreme Court's opinion in *SFFA* suggests how we might envision a dignity-based admissions process by focusing on the unique characteristics of each applicant.

The Free Development of the Personality

Perhaps the most common way the law talks about human dignity is that it guarantees the full and free development of the personality.[22] Look at how this idea is written into the law in different countries. The Spanish Constitution proclaims that "the dignity of the person, the inviolable rights which are inherent, the free development of the personality, the respect for the law and for the rights of others are the foundation of political order and social peace."[23] The Italian Constitution imposes on the state the obligation to remove obstacles that "constrain the freedom and equality of citizens, thereby impeding the full development of the human person."[24]

Courts use this language too. In a case about the rights of people in a same-sex relationship to adopt a child, the Supreme Court of Mexico said that "it is an absolutely fundamental right for the human being, the basis and condition of all others: the right to be recognized always as a human person. Thus, from human dignity, all other rights are released, insofar as they are necessary for man to fully develop his personality. [It is the] right to be recognized and to live in and with the dignity proper to the human person."[25]

Dignity consciousness values the development of the personality and the telling of one's unique life story in the way the *SFFA* Court mapped out. But the US Court itself failed to see the whole person whose interests are at issue and in so doing, it missed a precious opportunity to highlight how education is central to a person's free development, and how, by expanding access to education, the law can facilitate, not impede, the ability of each person to fully develop, thrive, and realize their life project.

Different Ways of Getting to Equality

"All human beings are born free and equal in dignity and rights." These are the opening words of the Universal Declaration of Human Rights. They suggest something critically important about equality and dignity, words that are often paired but are not synonymous. Dignity refers to the quality of human worth.

Equality ensures that each person's worth is equivalent. Dignity must be absolutely equal in each one of us for it to mean anything at all. Equal dignity means that no one has the power or the authority to measure another person's worth; no one can say that someone else's dignity is not worth as much or that one person's life is worth less than another's. If the door is opened even one tiny iota to the possibility that one person has more dignity than another, then any human rights abuse becomes possible in the name of that person's greater value.

But equal dignity does not mean that we are all identical. All people have equal worth, but no two people are the same. Dignity consciousness fully acknowledges the uniqueness of each person's character and circumstances. This is why the Court is on the right track when it encourages each person to tell their own story, including their individual sense of the meaning of race, or gender, or religion, in their own lives. And yet, the Court has always adhered to a view of equality that is formal rather than substantive. The rule of color-blindness itself is a formalist rule that treats everyone equally—as if they had no race. It takes no account of the differences—in real life—between different people and their different situations.

In many countries facing histories of rank discrimination, the concept of dignity provides a way to think about achieving greater equality in society. It can even provide a transformative engine for getting there. We see this in the Indian Court's treatment of education as key to the establishment of a post-caste society. Millions of Indians were given lower-caste status before India became an independent nation, and they, and their descendants, now live in "pitiable conditions" that the government is obligated to find ways to remedy:

> The aim of the Constitution is to equip each member of the
> weaker sections with the ability to compete with other citizens

with dignity on a level playing field. The pitiable condition of
Scheduled Castes is recognized by the Constitution as a national
problem. Therefore, the responsibility of improving the lot of
Scheduled Castes has been entrusted to the National Commission and the Parliament.[26]

The obligation is not to be blind to the caste system of
the past, or to avoid or ignore or deny present social and economic inequalities, and it does not matter that the current
government or even the current state is not responsible for
the inequalities of the past: if there are inequities, people are
suffering and the government must address them in some effective way. Being blind to injustice is not an option, nor is
creating formal rules that obscure reality and limit remedies.
The Indian Court entrusts to the state the choice of adopting
the most effective means of responding to ongoing legacies of
the caste system, which may include correction of the specific
problems.

The Canadian approach provides another illustration.
Though Canada did not engage in centuries of antiblack oppression, it does have a legacy of oppression against native
people that it is trying to wrestle with (as well as various forms
of discrimination on the basis of gender, religion, and nationality). Its 1982 Charter of Rights and Freedoms encourages such
transformation. Section 15(1) guarantees legal equality: "Every
individual is equal before and under the law and has the right
to the equal protection and equal benefit of the law without
discrimination." This ensures that every person stands as an
equal person before the law, similar to the US Equal Protection Clause. Section 15(2), however, opens the door for affirmative efforts aimed at protecting the dignity of all. It clarifies
that the first section "does not preclude any law, program or
activity that has as its object the amelioration of conditions

of disadvantaged individuals or groups including those that are disadvantaged because of race, national or ethnic origin, colour, religion, sex, age or mental or physical disability."[28] In Canada, as in India, all tools necessary to remedy rank discrimination of the past are available now. Discrimination and ameliorating discrimination are two different things, not two wrongs of the same ilk.

Rejecting US-style formalism, the Canadian Supreme Court reads these two provisions "as working together to promote substantive equality," which, it says, is "grounded in the idea that: The promotion of equality entails the promotion of a society in which all are secure in the knowledge that they are recognized at law as human beings equally deserving of concern, respect and consideration."[29] To accomplish this, the Court distinguishes discrimination (banned under s. 1), from an "ameliorative program aimed at combatting disadvantage" (permitted under s. 2).[30] In other words, the Canadian equal protection clauses do not eliminate race from the conversation but give the government the tools it needs to protect each person's dignity.[31]

The courts in Colombia have done the same. Recognizing equality "as a principle, as a value, and as a fundamental right," the Constitutional Court has insisted that this "goes much further than the classical formulation of equality before the law, to move toward the realization of conditions of material equality. Under this perspective," the Court continues, "a central proposition of the equality clause is the protection of groups that have been traditionally discriminated against or marginalized." The Court has further explained that this protection entails both the negative obligations (the "mandate of abstention or prohibition of discriminatory treatment") and a positive "mandate of intervention, in which the State is obligated to fulfill actions tend-ing to improve the conditions of material inequality that these groups face."[32] The government not only can but must use every available tool to remedy past discrimination, including both negative and affirmative action.

To effectively address continuing inequalities in America, we need to get way past the idea that the only harm of America's racist past was color-consciously "sorting" and that color-blindness will eliminate inequality. We need to confront the fact of ongoing deep and widespread social and economic inequality discernible along racial lines and recognize the government's obligation to act affirmatively to reduce these inequalities.

The Right to One's Uniqueness

The dignity right to one's uniqueness has two aspects. First, government must treat every person as an individual, not as a member of a group. Relatedly, government must treat each person as a person, with unique attributes.

The Right to Individualized Treatment

Although the reference to dignity in *SFFA* is brief, it touches on something important and meaningful both as a matter of inherent human worth and as a matter of public policy. The Court simply said that "it demeans the dignity and worth of a person to be judged by ancestry." In rejecting attention to the category of "race," it insisted that government make decisions that impact people based on their individual circumstances, not on their membership in or association with a particular abstract classification.[33]

Here we are concerned with the process of decision-making and whether the government takes into account the unique and individual aspects of each individual's personhood as a requirement of dignity law. Courts committed to human dignity often insist on individualized treatment. In a case about mass evictions of people from their homesteads, the great South African jurist Albie Sachs insisted that the landowners and the squatters engage in meaningful mediation.

> Thus, those seeking eviction should be encouraged not to rely on concepts of faceless and anonymous squatters automatically to be expelled as obnoxious social nuisances. Such a stereotypical approach has no place in the society envisaged by the Constitution; justice and equity require that everyone is to be treated as an individual bearer of rights entitled to respect for his or her dignity.[34]

It is this insistence on individualized assessment of a person's actual circumstances that caused the German Constitutional Court to prohibit preventive detention under its constitutional Basic Law.

> The offender may only be sentenced to imprisonment and subjected to its execution for the culpable commission of a wrong. This is based on the Basic Law's image of humanity, which is of a person capable of free self-determination; consideration is to be given to this image in the principle of blameworthiness rooted in human dignity.[35]

Even in the United States, this aspect of dignity that demands individual assessment is recognized, particularly in the criminal law where the burdens are so great. The Supreme Court has explained that mandatory death sentences are unconstitutional on this basis:

> We believe that, in capital cases, the fundamental respect for humanity underlying the Eighth Amendment requires consideration of the character and record of the individual offender and the circumstances of the particular offense.[36]

The same is true for mandatory life without parole sentences for minors.

> A line of our precedents, demanding individualized sentencing when imposing the death penalty [is relevant here. Certain deci-

sions] have elaborated on the requirement that capital defendants have an opportunity to advance, and the judge or jury a chance to assess, any mitigating factors, so that the death penalty is reserved only for the most culpable defendants committing the most serious offenses.[37]

This is especially important in the criminal arena where the burdens on a person are matters of life and death. But the essential premise operates equally throughout the law. When the *SFFA* Court derides giving "a tip" to people because they are part of a group or category of people rather than evaluate their individual situations and characteristics, it is upholding the imperative of individualized treatment that a dignity-based system demands.

The Right to Respect for Each Person's Uniqueness

The obligation to treat every person as a person is complemented by the obligation to respect each person's individuality or uniqueness. For instance, in the 2023 case from the Mexican Supreme Court about the right to terminate a pregnancy, the Court explained that the right to human dignity "recognizes a unique and exceptional quality to every human being for the simple fact of being so, whose full effectiveness must be respected and protected integrally and without exception."[38]

There is a wide range of dignity cases from around the world that underscores the need for government to respect each person's unique personhood. We see this often in cases involving sexual and gender identity, where the law accords each person the right to decide essential elements of their identity by and for themselves. In 2002, the European Court of Human Rights, sitting as a Grand Chamber, decided *Christine Goodwin v. The United Kingdom*, a case involving the rights of transsexuals. It held that since "the very essence of the [European Convention on Human Rights] is respect for human dignity and human freedom . . . where the notion of personal autonomy is an important principle underlying the interpretation of its guarantees, protection is given to the personal sphere of each individual, including the right to establish details of their identity as individual human beings."[39]

Similarly, the Indian Supreme Court, in recognizing the legal status of people who identify as "third gender," held that "each person's self-defined sexual orientation and gender identity is integral to their personality and is one of the most basic aspects of self-determination, dignity and freedom."[40] Citing several older decisions, the Court reiterated that "the right to dignity forms an essential part of our constitutional culture which seeks to ensure the full development and evolution of persons and includes 'expressing oneself in diverse forms, freely moving about and mixing and comingling with fellow human beings.'"[41] Gender and sexual identity, like race, should be defined by each person for themselves, as a matter of their own inherent dignity and in keeping with their own life project. Government authorities making assumptions about people because they are part of an abstract category is an ultimate form of objectification, particularly where assumptions are both conclusive and consequential.

The right to recognition for one's unique personality does more than allow people to self-identify; it imposes an obligation to do so—to self-define, to express oneself, to advocate for recognition of oneself as an individual. This approach also tracks the South African evictions case, which provides additional insight into the value of individual agency and control over one's own narrative. In requiring mediation between the landowners and the squatters, the South African court imposed a burden not only on the landowners to eschew stereotypes and to treat each squatter as an individual person but also on the persons needing a home to advocate for themselves. The Court explained:

> At the same time those who find themselves compelled by poverty
> and landlessness to live in shacks on the land of others, should be
> discouraged from regarding themselves as helpless victims, lack-
> ing the possibilities of personal moral agency. The tenacity and in-
> genuity they show in making homes out of discarded material, in
> finding work and sending their children to school, are a tribute to
> their capacity for survival and adaptation.[42]

Dignity is a two-way street. The government must respect it, and the applicant must claim it. The process laid out by the South African Court gives those seeking a place to live the opportunity to advocate for themselves and to show how their own merit, skills, and experiences qualify them for the kind of housing they seek. Each one should have the opportunity to present "as a person." Likewise, *SFFA* invites each applicant to show "how race affected his or her life, be it through discrimination, inspiration, or otherwise," or how they "overcame racial discrimination," or how their "heritage or culture motivated him or her to assume a leadership role or attain a particular goal."[43] This process puts each applicant in charge of how they present themselves to the admissions committee, not as one of thousands who checked a box or as a victim of someone else's narrative, but as a person with a full set of unique life experiences with full control over the story of their lives. It may in this way advance human dignity: to earn the privilege of admission not because of membership in a group but on the basis of one's own unique personhood. This opportunity for agency and individuation has always existed in the application process but may be heightened now with the attention the Supreme Court has given to it.

A Missed Opportunity to Promote Human Dignity

The question of affirmative action in twenty-first-century America raises a host of complex and interlocking issues. The Supreme Court has never done a good job of elucidating the issues or providing a framework for thinking about them or a vocabulary for discussing them. Maybe that's not its job, though courts in some countries have used their intellectual resources and the authority they wield in society to do just that. Even in the United States, the purpose of a Supreme Court opinion is not only to announce who wins and who loses but to explain the principles that inform the Court's reasoning. In *SFFA*, various members of the Court collectively wrote nearly 250 pages but they still failed to help us understand what to do about our history of racial oppression and the present reality of racial inequality and social injustice in America.

In slamming the door on race-conscious admissions decision-making, the *SFFA* Court may have opened the door to more individually personalized and holistic decision-making by admissions officers who seek to foster diverse learning environments. They can still accomplish their diversity goals, but they must do so by examining the whole and nuanced narrative of each applicant, not just by looking at the box they checked. (For those admissions officers who were doing that before, this opinion will not change much.)

Whether or not race consciousness has worked or is necessary, it is surely not the only way to advance goals of equity and inclusion in higher education or in society more generally. University scholarships to students who are from underresourced communities or who are the first in their families to go to college may accomplish similar goals. Likewise, it is quite possible that giving contract preferences to businesses that are undercapitalized or whose owners are first-generation businesspeople would be at least as effective in reducing racial inequities than set-asides to minority-owned businesses per se. Taking into account each applicant's inherent human dignity may actually do more to reduce racial inequity and advance social justice than simple race consciousness.

This is not to say that racism in America isn't a wicked problem. It is and continues to be, for myriad reasons. But if we focus on the expansion of human dignity as the ultimate goal, we at least aim at the target we are trying to hit.

THREE

The Dignity in Reproductive Rights

Competing Claims for Dignity Rights? Not Necessarily

Abortion is a uniquely difficult problem both for necessary and unnecessary reasons. Abortion is necessarily a serious issue because there is hardly anything that affects a woman's dignity— her life, her health, her body, her autonomy, and so forth—more than the decision concerning whether to have a child. And the decision to terminate a pregnancy is not only self-regarding but ends the developing life of another. No other social controversy gives the claimant such a strong dignity right, and in no other situation is there such a direct countervailing claim to protection from another human. (Compared with affirmative action, for instance, the claim to the right to admission does not have the same force and the countervailing rejection from a university does not do the same degree of damage to an applicant.)

But in the United States, conversations about abortion are often complicated and distorted by political and religious rhetoric that obfuscates the reality of reproductive rights and drives the dialogue away from the facts and to the extremes of hyperbole. Arguments about the "right to life," rooted in American Catholic doctrine and developed by the political right, are now engraved into American constitutional law. These reasons are unnecessary in the sense that they are not intrinsic to abortion or to American constitutional law. Indeed, other lenses produce a different result. International human rights law recognizes the dignity of every person *born* a member of the human family, as the Universal Declaration of Human Rights says. Some countries, including countries whose populations are predominantly Catholic, have resolved the abortion issue in ways that are consonant with women's dignity.[1] And even in the United States, at least one state Supreme Court has found the rights to control over one's body and to self-determination are inalienable rights rooted both in natural law and constitutional text.[2]

The United States Supreme Court has taken a decidedly different view. In 2022, the Court reversed fifty years of limited protection for the reproductive rights of women when it decided, in *Dobbs v. Jackson Women's Health Organization*, that ending a pregnancy is not a "liberty" interest protected by the US Constitution. "Guided by the history and tradition that map the essential components of the Nation's concept of ordered liberty," the Court said, "the clear answer is that the Fourteenth Amendment does not protect the right to an abortion." Without any constitutional mandate, states are free to regulate abortion as they see fit. This sounds like a pro-democracy "let the people decide" decision. But it instantly put the lives and health of thirty-four million women at risk and impeded the availability of and access to abortion for many more. Some of these women join the ninety million women of reproductive age worldwide who live in countries such as Laos, Malta, Honduras, Senegal, and Egypt, where abortion is banned.[3] By contrast, women throughout Europe and the Americas can legally and effectively obtain abortions.[4]

There is simply no way to summarize access to abortion in

the United States since *Dobbs*. State legislatures, which are over-whelmingly male,[5] have been extremely creative in developing obstacles to women's reproductive autonomy. In the immediate aftermath of *Dobbs*, some states legislatively ensured that abortion would remain legal, while many others adopted some kinds of restrictions or total bans. Even where abortion is legal, it is not available in much of the country, particularly in rural areas—which is most of the nation. And even if it is legal and available, certain restrictions, like twenty-four-hour waiting periods or pregnancy duration limits, may make it impossible for girls and women to obtain abortions, delay the health care they need, increase the cost, and magnify their vulnerability. The Center for Reproductive Rights identifies seven types of bans, four types of abortion restrictions, and five types of regulations regarding abortion access (relating to public funding, private insurance requirements, clinic safety and access, abortion provider qualifications, and interstate shields), all of which may be in effect, partially effective, or enjoined at any given time. In the sixteen months following *Dobbs*, fourteen states have total bans in effect.[6] The post-*Dobbs* landscape leaves women without the equal protection of the law and therefore vulnerable to exploitation, legal entanglements, and risks to their health and lives. Mostly, it fails to protect the inherent and equal dignity of women and girls.

Early estimates indicate that "in the first six months of 2023, births rose by an average of 2.3 percent in states enforcing total abortion bans compared to a control group of states where abortion rights remained protected, amounting to approximately 32,000 additional annual births resulting from abortion bans."[7] These effects were not uniform: the increases in births "tend to be larger for younger women and women of color" and happened most often in Texas and Mississippi.

Of course, from the perspective of those who support *Dobbs*, that is precisely the point. If abortion is murder, then the only rational policy is to prohibit it. There are exceptions to the prohibition against killing a human being in the United States, but they mostly involve killing a person who has done something wrong, as in the case of capital punishment or self-defense, or people may subject themselves to the risk of death in the name of some important national policy objective as in the case of war. Clearly, fetuses have done nothing wrong and have not chosen to put their lives on the line. And if some form of personhood begins before birth, then it may be appropriate to say at least some rights do too. That said, it must also be recognized that while live births may have increased after *Dobbs*, so has infant mortality: one study in Texas found that "in 2022, the year after the state's six-week abortion ban took effect, deaths of infants before their first birthdays increased 13 percent," and the number of babies born with life-threatening congenital conditions who died "rose 23 percent in that period, compared with a 3 percent decrease in the rest of the country." The results "suggest that additional live births occurring in Texas in 2022 disproportionately included pregnancies at increased risk of infant mortality, particularly those involving congenital anomalies."[8]

So how to accommodate both views? Where dignity-respecting countries have landed is pretty much where the Supreme Court landed in 1973 when it decided *Roe v. Wade*: the woman's claim to control her life is compelling throughout pregnancy, but the fetal claim to life changes as it develops. Early on, it is not significant enough to challenge her dignity right, but at some point, the fetal claim to life and to be treated as a person with dignity may limit the woman's decision-making autonomy. Another way of saying this is that courts have permitted restrictions on abortion only if they respect women's dignity. Indeed, this was the holding of the Supreme Court of Kansas in 2019.

How Courts Talk about the Dignity of Reproductive Choice

When courts around the world have considered questions of reproductive rights including abortion, they've often done so through the lens of human dignity. This focuses attention on the impacts of reproductive health on the lived experiences of those who are facing decisions about motherhood and family planning.

Dignity, American Style

Before *Roe* was overturned but while its death was foretold, the Kansas Supreme Court issued a remarkable opinion upholding the right to terminate a pregnancy (or at least requiring courts to strictly scrutinize laws that conflict with that right, with the likely result that such laws would be invalidated). At issue in the case was a state law that prohibited a type of abortion procedure most commonly used in the second trimester. Two doctors claimed that it violated the natural rights provision that opens the Kansas Bill of Rights: "All men are possessed of equal and inalienable natural rights, among which are life, liberty, and the pursuit of happiness." The Court's eighty-seven-page opinion—wending through the Magna Carta, Locke and Burke, and the history of the state's 1859 Constitution against the backdrop of antislavery debates, and more—finds that the Constitution protects for all people certain essential natural rights that people have not only because they are enumerated in a legal text but by virtue of their humanity.

> At the core of the natural rights of liberty and the pursuit of happiness is the right of personal autonomy, which includes the ability to control one's own body, to assert bodily integrity, and to exercise self-determination. This ability enables decision-making about issues that affect one's physical health, family formation, and family life. Each of us has the right to make self-defining and self-governing decisions about these matters.[9]

Indeed, the Court finds that numerous other state constitutions also protect natural rights and also in these terms of bodily control and decisional autonomy and self-determination.[10] Then the Court closes the loop, recognizing that what it describes as the inalienable natural right of personal autonomy is "the heart of human dignity" and that the decisions that dignity protects "can include whether to continue a pregnancy."[11]

The Court then holds that, given the importance of the right at issue, any law infringing on it must satisfy a legal standard known as strict scrutiny, which places the burden on those justifying the law to prove that the law is necessary to accomplish a compelling state interest. On remand, the district court recognized the state's interest in protecting the "value and dignity of human life, born and unborn" but found that prohibiting this particular form of abortion was not necessary to accomplish it.

As we will see, the Kansas Supreme Court's understanding of dignity, while distinctly American in its reliance on the natural rights thinking of Enlightenment philosophers like John Locke, tracks surprisingly closely with the dignity-based approaches of courts in other parts of the world on the issue of abortion. Some of these most recent decisions have been in direct response to *Dobbs*.

A few months after the US Supreme Court decided to leave women's right to choose unprotected, the Supreme Court of India issued a landmark decision respecting women's right to choose; Mexico followed suit a few months later in 2023. These cases complemented the amendment to the French Constitution, in 2024, to protect abortion rights, in a direct rebuke to the American experience.[12] The Indian and Mexican cases are worth examining at length because they show how the abortion issue can be framed as a matter of human dignity. Of course, the courts think about these issues in the context of their own countries' culture and values and traditions, which are different from some American values. But it turns out that the way the courts talk about what is fundamentally important to people is not very different at all from what we in America think is important. So we can learn from their approach and the language they use to think about our own social controversies, like abortion, in a new way.

India: The Right to Live with Dignity

The Indian case involved a twenty-five-year old woman who became pregnant as the result of a consensual relationship: "She did not want to carry the pregnancy to term since she was wary of the 'social stigma and harassment' pertaining to unmarried single parents," and without a reliable source of income, "she was not mentally prepared to 'raise and nurture the child as an unmarried mother.'"[13] The Court held that the law banning abortions under these circumstances was unconstitutional.

The Supreme Court of India has, since the 1980s, interpreted the constitutional protection for the right to life (in Article 21 of the Indian Constitution) as the right to live with dignity. Although it is not written into the text, the Court has said that the Constitution was designed to ensure not just that people could live or exist but could live their lives with dignity.

This is not too different from the US Supreme Court saying, in the 1960s, that the right to liberty has to mean more than the right just not to be locked up without due process of law but includes certain values within the zone of each person's privacy: in the United States, the constitutional guarantee of liberty means that government cannot encroach on the most intimate and private aspects of personhood, such as whom to marry, whether to have children, and how to raise them.[14] But while the US Court was, for decades, expansive in its reading of the *liberty* guarantee, it has never interpreted the *life* guarantee to mean anything other than the right not to be put to death without due process of law. But if in the United States we thought of the meaning of "life" more robustly, it might very well look like the right to live with dignity.

In the Indian abortion case, the Court explains the background principles: "Dignity has been recognized as a core component of the right to life and liberty under Article 21. . . . The right to dignity encapsulates the right of every individual to be treated as a self-governing entity having intrinsic value. It means that every human being possesses dignity merely by being a human, and can make self-defining and self-determining choices."[15]

The Court then applies these principles to the situation of a person who seeks to end a pregnancy. First, it focuses on the aspect of abortion that entails control over one's body and the decisional agency over one's life.

> If women with unwanted pregnancies are forced to carry their pregnancies to term, the state would be stripping them of the right to determine the immediate and long-term path their lives would take. Depriving women of autonomy not only over their bodies but also over their lives would be an affront to their dignity. The right to choose for oneself—be it as significant as choosing the course of one's life or as mundane as one's day-to-day activities—forms a part of the right to dignity. It is this right which would be under attack if women were forced to continue with unwanted pregnancies.[16]

Remember, if dignity means anything, it is the authority of each person to control their own life. If anyone decides what course your life should take, to suit their own ends, they are objectifying you, forcing you to submit to their will. This can happen in the case of a child, whose parent may decide where the child goes to school and maybe even what the child eats and whom the child plays with. But even here there are limits, such as respecting the bodily integrity of the child by prohibiting physical harm to the child and obliging the parent to provide nutrition and safety to the child. These are based in the child's dignity. The same limits apply with adults who are, for one reason or another, deemed incompetent and rely on others to make decisions and care for them. But in the case of a competent adult, it is up to that person, and no one else, to control their life course.

The Court then focuses even more closely on the aspect of dignity that protects decision-making.

> In the context of abortion, the right to dignity entails recognising the competence and authority of every woman to take reproductive decisions, including the decision to terminate the pregnancy. Although human dignity inheres in every individual, it is susceptible to violation by external conditions and treatment imposed by the state. The right of every woman to make reproductive choices without undue interference from the state is central to the idea of human dignity. Deprivation of access to reproductive healthcare or emotional and physical well-being also injures the dignity of women.

If the authority to make decisions for oneself is essential to human dignity, then the government must ensure that decisions are informed and that choices are real. Look at how far the Indian Supreme Court goes to make sure that the decision to have an abortion is made absolutely freely:

> The state must ensure that information regarding reproduction and safe sexual practices is disseminated to all parts of the population. Further, it must see to it that all segments of society are able to access contraceptives to avoid unintended pregnancies and plan their families. Medical facilities . . . must be present in each district and must be affordable to all. The government must ensure that [medical facilities] treat all patients equally and sensitively. Treatment must not be denied on the basis of one's caste or due to other social or economic factors. It is only when these recommendations become a reality that we can say that the right to bodily autonomy and the right to dignity are capable of being realized.

Women in India have a legal right to make decisions for themselves, the same as men would have. Of course, many women in India face incredible discrimination and subjugation, but at least the law explicitly recognizes them as full autonomous individual human beings and the courts are working to assure that women have not only the right but the opportunity to experience the full scope of their dignity.

Mexico: The Right to Decisional Autonomy

Twelve months after the Indian case and fourteen months after *Dobbs*, the Supreme Court of Mexico issued its own landmark abortion decision. Following the Indian Supreme Court, but using its own language and approach, it, too, holds that abortion rights are essential to protecting human dignity.

Building on a previous opinion, the Court in the 2023 case explains that the right to reproductive autonomy of "women and people capable of gestating" results from a particular combination of "rights and principles associated with the intrinsic liberty of each person to decide for themselves (auto-determination) and to freely choose the options and circumstances that give meaning to their existence, according to their own convictions."[17]

In a section of the opinion devoted to human dignity, the Court explains why dignity is the fundamental value of the constitutional state even though (as in the United States) it is not explicit in the text.

> Human dignity is not just a simple ethical declaration, but consecrates a fundamental personal right which imposes on every governmental authority a mandate to respect and protect the dignity of every human being, understood—in its essence—as the inherent interest of each individual, by the mere fact of being a human being, to be treated as such and not as an object, to not be humiliated, degraded, debased, or objectified.[18]

The Court then applies these principles to abortion. Human dignity, the Court says, recognizes the particularities of pregnancy and is founded in the idea that "women and people with the capacity to gestate can freely use their bodies and can develop their identities and their destinies autonomously, free of obstacles, which is part of recognizing the elements that define them and the exercise of their rights necessary for the full development of their life."[19]

In Mexico, the Court found that abortion restrictions not only limit the ability of women to control their lives but also constrain women's ability to make important decisions for themselves. The Court refers to such limitations on women's decision-making autonomy as "paternalism," which reflects the idea that women need to be "protected" from their own decisions about their life choices and their reproductive and sexual health and disregards that women are rational and autonomous individuals, fully capable of making decisions for themselves.[20]

These two countries—from vastly different religious traditions, in different regions of the world, with different social and economic needs and resources, with different judicial histories and legal structures, and different forms of gender oppression— reach exactly the same conclusion about abortion: the right to choose is protected as a dignity right because governments *must* protect the ability of each person to make important life decisions for herself, to control her own body, fully develop her personality, and control her own life course.

But how do we use this language to thread the needle through the abortion debate in the United States?

Applying Lessons from Abroad

Interestingly, these ideas in precisely this language can be found in various places in the United States. The Constitution of Vermont protects "personal reproductive liberty" this way:

Vermont Constitution. Article 22. [Personal reproductive liberty]

That an individual's right to personal reproductive autonomy is central to the liberty and dignity to determine one's own life course and shall not be denied or infringed unless justified by a compelling State interest achieved by the least restrictive means.

So the language of dignity exists in the United States. But how do we build on it to galvanize a real national conversation about abortion? If we want a policy about abortion rights that advances human dignity, what can we learn from our friends in places as diverse as India, Mexico—and Vermont and Kansas?

First, we can see that dignity is important. A constitutional system that ignores dignity—whether or not it's written into the text—is ignoring the very purpose of constitutional government. A constitution's purpose is to expand human freedom by limiting state power. Dignity is the twenty-first century's way of talking about freedom. So, when written or read into a constitution, dignity demarcates the line between governmental power and the untouchable realm of individual identity and autonomy that is essential to human freedom. This is why it is implied even in constitutions where it is not explicit, such as those of India and Mexico or Kansas for that matter. It is a non-derogable duty on the part of the state to restrict its own power to protect every person's essential humanity.

Second, when we talk about dignity, we are talking about a constellation of interrelated and interdependent rights: the right to make decisions for oneself, the right to plan one's life course, the right to bodily integrity and control, and so on. Together, these go to the essence of a person's identity and sense of self-worth. Because these are the rights most directly affected by abortion laws, dignity rights protect against excessively limiting abortion restrictions. This is the essence of the *Dobbs'* dissenters' rebuke of the majority:

A majority of today's Court has wrenched reproductive choice from women and given it to the States. To allow a State to exert control over one of "the most intimate and personal choices" a woman may make is not only to affect the course of her life, monumental as those effects might be. It is to alter her "views of [herself]" and her understanding of her "place[] in society" as someone with the recognized dignity and authority to make these choices. Women have relied on *Roe* and *Casey* in this way for 50 years. Many have never known anything else. When *Roe* and *Casey* disappear, the loss of power, control, and dignity will be immense.[21]

Third, these interests are not just psychological or ephemeral. They go directly to a person's ability to live with dignity, in all its dimensions. Dignity touches on and reinforces other rights, so abortion restrictions need to be understood as affecting a person's ability to work or to go to school, and that affects many other rights associated with living a life of dignity.

Fourth, abortion restrictions affect a woman's right to *equal* dignity, in two important and independent ways. They impede her right to control her body, and to control her life course, as any man has the right to. This is why the International Convention on the Elimination of All Forms of Discrimination Against Women recognizes that reproductive autonomy is violated when there are obstacles to women's ability to control if and when they have children.[22] Just as perniciously, abortion restrictions, including restrictions on the reasons for obtaining an abortion, paternalistically make the decision *for* the woman as if her decision-making ability has to be checked. This is equally paternalistic and equally offensive to human dignity whether it is the state or another person who decides for a person what she should do when she becomes pregnant.

And fifth, to talk about dignity is to talk about human beings. It isn't about abstractions, even meaningful ones. To judge with dignity is to judge with empathy for people whose experiences are different from—and sometimes much, much more challenging than—the judge's own. It is about the ways that rules have a day-to-day impact on how we live, how we feel, what life choices are possible. The US Supreme Court's fixation on "history" and "tradition" (as the *Dobbs* Court insisted) disclaims, in the dissent's language, "any need to consider broad swaths of individuals' interests."[23] No one lives in a world of history or tradition or of "justice" and "liberty" (two other talismanic words to which the Court clings). And certainly no one lives in a world of originalism. No, people live in a world where they wake up one morning and find they are pregnant and have to figure out what to do; they live ten hours from the nearest reproductive health-care clinic and cannot take time off from work; and they are feeling nauseous and do not have money to pay the caregiver for the toddler; and so on and so forth. These are women's lives, the lives that are impacted, in real and very concrete ways, by laws that limit women's options and make it harder for them to live with dignity. The Court's approach ignores real life.

So we have to contend with the fact that prohibiting abortion will not eliminate the interruption of pregnancy or the protection of infant life. Women and girls will get abortions if they need to whether or not they are legal and whether or not they are safe. (Some early reports indicate that while the birth rate has gone up due to the unavailability of abortion in some places, the abortion rate has gone up in other places.) The riskier it is to get an abortion, the more infants will be born into lives without dignity and without even the hope of survival. That is a reality that the pro-life forces have not fully confronted. So the real question in the abortion debate is not whether America should tolerate abortion in the abstract but whether women and girls will have safe and legal reproductive health care that will protect their dignity or whether their reproductive health care will put their lives at risk, increase their vulnerabilities, and subject them to criminal liability.

Dignity-speak is forward-looking, progressive, and potentially transformative. The *Dobbs* Court's fixation on history and tradition is not only out of sync with how people live; it is out of sync with its global peers' attention to human dignity, and out of sync with how we should think about what kinds of laws we want. Courts that have focused on dignity often use it with social transformation in mind, to pivot from the past to the future. This is obviously the meaning of dignity in the Universal Declaration of Human Rights, adopted while the embers of World War II were still burning, to establish a new world order in which the horrors of the war would never again be repeated. It is one of the reasons dignity appears so prevalently in the constitutional orders of the newly established postcolonial, postdictatorship, postcommunist, and postwar states. It is the reason that the European Court of Human Rights seized on the concept in its 1995 decision outlawing—for the first time ever—marital rape: the husband had argued that he had a right to rape his wife because men have always had that right. The Court vehemently disagreed: in the modern world, defined by a commitment to human dignity, rape is never permissible and, the Court said, men's control over their wives has to end.[24] It's the reason that Justice Anthony Kennedy used dignity in his decisions on same-sex relations, including *Lawrence v. Texas* (2003), *Windsor v. United States* (2013), and *Obergefell v. Hodges* (2015). A dignity lens is one way to transition toward a world in which all people to have full agency over their lives and have the right to live with dignity.

What about Fetal Interests and the Potentiality of Life?

In a way, the balance between women's dignity on the one hand and fetal interests and the potentiality of life on the other is a false dichotomy. As mentioned, restricting abortion does not necessarily protect fetal life because women will have abortions anyway if they are needed. But even assuming some restrictions do save lives, the countervailing interests of the fetus are complicated. Different people, adhering to different traditions and different conceptions of those traditions, have differing opinions about when the right to life, and to dignity, begins. Religious groups have weighed in on both sides,[25] just as atheists have. So turning to religion for a rule restricting abortion is inconclusive, runs counter to a commitment to dignity, and threatens the sectional pluralism that is central to the American conception of religious liberty.

Rachel Bayevsky writes about how attention to dignity can nonetheless contribute to a more meaningful conversation.

> Given that dignity is invoked on multiple sides of abortion disputes, one might wonder what dignity has to offer to the law. Dignity offers a language that opposing parties can both use to express strongly held positions.
>
> In particular, dignity could provide a means of acknowledging the moral seriousness of parties' differing positions. Perhaps it is not inherently contradictory to recognize both the dignity of fetal life (or potential life) and the dignity of women. On this understanding, characterizing interests in dignitary terms could demonstrate a degree of respect for the cultural and moral understandings that inform (even if they do not determine) divergent legal positions. . . .
>
> In invoking dignity, participants in these debates are giving voice to divergent normative perspectives. We should not expect the underlying normative disagreement to disappear. Yet appeals to dignity could facilitate a more focused collision of perspectives, centered on the question of which practices best further dignitary goals, and for whom.[26]

Dignity does manifest the moral gravitas of the situation. Under international law and for most courts, recognizing human dignity, including the dignity of a pregnant person, guarantees an inviolable right and forces the state to achieve its objects without compromising that right. It is not subject to balancing, to proportionality testing, or to any kind of limitation. Just as there can be no exceptions for the dignity-based prohibition on rape or torture, there can be no exceptions to the dignity-based right to reproductive autonomy. This does not mean that abortions must be permitted at all times and in all circumstances. But it does mean that whatever protections are put in place for fetal life must be consistent with the woman's dignity. A restriction may limit her choice, but it's invalid if it limits her dignity.

Decisions with Empathy

Attention to human dignity doesn't necessarily tell us all the answers. It doesn't tell us how many weeks is the right number to allow some restrictions on abortion or when a doctor's intervention is needed. But it tells us what questions to ask. It requires us to develop policies that respect the dignity of all people under all circumstances. It requires us to protect the core of the human self, where one feels one's sense of worth, where one has the sense of agency over one's life and can make decisions for oneself according to the dictates of one's conscience. It also compels a certain empathy toward others, based in the realization that each of us has equal dignity and in the obligation, as the UDHR and the American Declaration of the Rights and Duties of Man both say, that we should act toward one another as brothers and sisters.

FOUR

Drawing a Dignity Line between
Free Speech and Hate Speech

Hate Speech in the Marketplace of Ideas

On August 11 and 12, 2017, a far-right rally was held in Charlottesville, Virginia—the home of the University of Virginia and
Thomas Jefferson and the symbolic cradle of free speech in American academia; on the downtown Mall, there is a "Free Speech
Wall" on which people are invited to express themselves just for
the sake of free expression. In some versions, what happened in
Charlottesville was an example of free speech, harkening back to
the 1977 cases in which federal and state courts held that neo-Nazi
groups had a right to march in the town of Skokie, Illinois, specifically chosen because it was home to a large population of Jewish
people who had survived the Holocaust. Fast-forward forty-five
years to Charlottesville, where modern-day Nazis and members
of the modern-day Ku Klux Klan and other white supremacist
groups gathered together under the banner of "Unite the Right"
to make a show of power, just as their grandparents' generation
had done in Illinois. The racism and supremacist ideology of

the marchers was unmistakable: showing their true colors, they held swastikas and Confederate flags and chanted, among other things, "You will not replace us," referring to "the popular white supremacist belief that the white race is in danger of extinction by a rising tide of non-Whites who are controlled and manipulated by Jews (in fact, one variant of 'You Will Not Replace Us' is 'Jews Will Not Replace Us')," according to the Anti-Defamation League.[1]

Embodying classic free-speech values, a coalition of counterprotesters emerged to "remedy" the hate speech with their own antiracist speech. But this produced not a healthy exchange of ideas but vitriolic and violent clashes: thirty people were injured and one person, Heather Heyer, whom friends described as "a passionate advocate for the disenfranchised who was often moved to tears by the world's injustices,"[2] was killed when a racist protestor rammed his car into a crowd of counterprotesters.

Let's leave Charlottesville and drive three hours north to the US Congress where, on December 5, 2023, Representative Elise Stefanik questioned the presidents of three elite universities about the protests occurring on college campuses over the war between Israel and Hamas. Repeatedly insisting on a yes-no answer, Representative Stefanik asked if calls for the genocide of Jews would violate their universities' codes of conduct. Much to the disconcertment of everyone, free-speech law in the United States cannot be reduced to a simple sound bite; it is full of rules, variations on rules, exceptions to rules, and thin slices carved out of the exceptions to the variations. So, like caricatures of overly thoughtful academics, the three intellectual elites hemmed and hawed and looked ridiculous in the public eye for failing to effectively and emphatically condemn calls for the genocide, of anyone, including Jews. No one lost their life, but all three of the presidents have by now lost their jobs.

In fact, there was a good and clear answer to the representative's question. But it isn't the one anyone wants to say or hear. Calls for genocide, like calls for anything else, are constitutionally protected in our society because a call is nothing more than words of advocacy, and advocacy of even the most heinous ideas is protected under the Constitution as long as it does not incite imminent lawless action.[3] That is why the Nazis can march in Skokie and in Charlottesville. That is why people can burn crosses and engage in all manner of hateful, hurtful, and harmful speech. That is why college students who want their universities to divest from Israel can set up encampments, wave flags, put up signs with messages that are offensive and hurtful to some, whether in solidarity with a cause or opposed to it. It's just speech, the courts tell us, and people can take it or leave it, respond to it or ignore it, counter it with loving speech or turn away. If people want to put hate speech in the marketplace of ideas, there it stays—up to the point where it crosses a line and becomes incitement of lawless action or a true threat or something like that.[4] Only at that point can a state ban it.

This chapter proposes a dignity-based approach to working through the problems posed by our nation's commitment to free speech.

The Dignity of Whitney: A Historical Framework

The most beautiful passages ever written by a Supreme Court justice (in my opinion), and the theoretical basis of our nation's ongoing commitment to free speech, is found in a 1927 case involving the conviction of Charlotte Anita Whitney. Whitney was from a very prominent family that included Eli Whitney, two Supreme Court justices, the geologist after whom Mount Whitney was named, and many wealthy financiers. Whitney herself may be the only member of her illustrious family who spent time in San Quentin, when she was convicted and sentenced to one to fourteen years for having helped establish the Communist Labor Party in California. A tireless advocate for racial and gender equality, workers' rights, and pacifism, both domestically and internationally, she was convicted of violating California's criminal syndicalism statute. This law, like many others adopted in the early twentieth century, prohibited membership in an organization that advocates "any doctrine or precept advocating, teaching or aiding and abetting the commission of crime, sabotage or unlawful acts of force and violence or unlawful methods of terrorism as a means of accomplishing a change in industrial ownership or control, or effecting any political change."[5] Although she vehemently denied any interest in violence, she was nonetheless convicted of violating the statute.

Justice Louis Brandeis agreed with the majority on the basis of a technical failure in her argument, but he took the occasion to express his views on the importance of free speech in the American democracy, even speech so harmful that a "vast majority" of a state's citizens "believes to be false and fraught with evil consequence." His exegesis on the limited power of the state to suppress even this speech is worth quoting at length:

> Those who won our independence believed that the final end of the State was to make men free to develop their faculties, and that, in its government, the deliberative forces should prevail over the arbitrary. They valued liberty both as an end, and as a means. They believed liberty to be the secret of happiness, and courage to be the secret of liberty. They believed that freedom to think as you will and to speak as you think are means indispensable to the discovery and spread of political truth; that, without free speech and assembly, discussion would be futile; that, with them, discussion affords ordinarily adequate protection against the dissemination of noxious doctrine; that the greatest menace to freedom is an inert people; that public discussion is a political duty, and that this should be a fundamental principle of the American government. They recognized the risks to which all human institutions are subject. But

they knew that order cannot be secured merely through fear of punishment for its infraction; that it is hazardous to discourage thought, hope and imagination; that fear breeds repression; that repression breeds hate; that hate menaces stable government; that the path of safety lies in the opportunity to discuss freely supposed grievances and proposed remedies, and that the fitting remedy for evil counsels is good ones. Believing in the power of reason as applied through public discussion, they eschewed silence coerced by law—the argument of force in its worst form. Recognizing the occasional tyrannies of governing majorities, they amended the Constitution so that free speech and assembly should be guaranteed.

Fear of serious injury cannot alone justify suppression of free speech and assembly. Men feared witches and burnt women. It is the function of speech to free men from the bondage of irrational fears. . . . Every denunciation of existing law tends in some measure to increase the probability that there will be violation of it. Condonation of a breach enhances the probability. Expressions of approval add to the probability. . . . But even advocacy of violation, however reprehensible morally, is not a justification for denying free speech where the advocacy falls short of incitement and there is nothing to indicate that the advocacy would be immediately acted on. The wide difference between advocacy and incitement, between preparation and attempt, between assembling and conspiracy, must be borne in mind. In order to support a finding of clear and present danger, it must be shown either that immediate serious violence was to be expected or was advocated, or that the past conduct furnished reason to believe that such advocacy was then contemplated.

Brandeis's language is pure poetry. But it is also profound and important. It sees freedom of speech in two interlocking dimensions at once. It is an individual value that makes people strong and fearless and that breeds thought, hope, and imagination. And it is also a social value that is essential for democracy and for a society that values liberty and freedom. For these reasons, we are committed to the largest and freest possible marketplace of ideas, where ideas are on offer to all passersby who can take them or leave them, or counter them with new ideas.

Only speech that creates a clear and present danger can be excluded from this speech bazaar.

This is precisely why even "calls for genocide," however morally reprehensible, are nonetheless protected in our constitutional system: although they may increase the likelihood of harm more than if they had not been said, they do not, *in and of themselves*, cause a clear and present danger. If harm ensues, it is not the speech itself that causes it but the intervening actions of listeners intent on doing harm and taking action that pose the actual danger. To punish the speakers is to act out of fear and cowardice, to be afraid of words and the ideas they convey.

Brandeis insists that the appropriate response to such calls is not to punish the speakers but to counter the speech, because the "fitting remedy for evil counsels is good ones." This is exactly what Heather Heyer and her fellow counterprotesters did in Charlottesville and what counterprotesters did on college campuses across America in May 2024. This is what universities should do when students or others express themselves in ways that contravene the university's values. This is why we don't hold President Trump accountable for the bomb threats in Springfield, Ohio, that followed his statements about immigrants there; we counter those statements to reveal the truth.[6]

In closing, Brandeis is even more clear:

> Those who won our independence by revolution were not cowards. They did not fear political change. They did not exalt order at the cost of liberty. To courageous, self-reliant men, with confidence in the power of free and fearless reasoning applied through the processes of popular government, no danger flowing from speech can be deemed clear and present unless the incidence of the evil apprehended is so imminent that it may befall before there is opportunity for full discussion. If there be time to expose through discussion the falsehood and fallacies, to avert the evil by the processes of education, the remedy to be applied is more speech, not

enforced silence. Only an emergency can justify repression. Such must be the rule if authority is to be reconciled with freedom.[7]

It took two generations, but Justice Brandeis's opinion finally won the day. In *Brandenburg v. Ohio*, the Supreme Court held that the state cannot punish someone for advocacy that falls short of incitement to illegal action.[8] That sounds like a victory for free speech, and it is. But it is also a victory for hate speech. Brandenburg himself was the local Ku Klux Klan leader and was prosecuted for a venom-filled racist and anti-Semitic rant as evil as anything we hear today. But like Brandenburg's speech, the chants uttered by Unite the Right, or President Trump's words about immigrants, though they may be false and fraught with evil consequence and are likely to increase the probability of real harm, do not typically meet the standard of incitement to *immediate* lawless action. Our Supreme Court has chosen, repeatedly, over decades, to protect such speech.

This approach to free speech has two problems: one is related to dignity, while the other goes to the very meaning of free speech. This tolerance of a broad band of speech, including hate speech, is good if you have a lot of hateful things to say; your speech is largely protected. It's not as good if you are on the receiving end of someone's hatred. And it's not especially good for society to have no guardrails on speech, especially in these times where any one of us can have a wider audience and broader influence on social media than the *New York Times* ever dreamed of. Fundamentally, it ignores the real harm that hateful speech causes, whether or not it leads to hateful action and violence. It's true that sticks and stones can break bones, but it's also true that words can't hurt only if you are invulnerable—that is, if you have wealth and the law and society's support on your side. If you are a part of a marginalized or disempowered community, words that seek to diminish and hurt you because of your race, nationality, religion, sexual or gender identity, or anything else can in fact harm you just by their very utterance. These things hurt precisely because they are aimed like an arrow directly at a person's dignity. They diminish your sense of self; damage the esteem in which others hold you; and, in insisting on your unworthiness, they reduce or eliminate your standing in your community. In fact, hate speech is damaging because it ultimately separates, isolates, and ostracizes a person from their community. You are not one of us, it says, in so many words. You don't belong here. Nothing says "get out" more clearly than two pieces of wood tied together to make a cross and set afire on the lawn of new neighbors—which is exactly what the Supreme Court upheld in its seminal cross-burning case, *R.A.V. v. St Paul*. At the extreme are calls for genocide, which aim to eliminate some people from the entire human race. That hate speech doesn't hurt you physically does not mean it doesn't hurt your dignity. The Supreme Court's jurisprudence—developed by men and a few women who are for the most part invulnerable—ignores the ways words can hurt.

The Difference between Hate Speech and Love Speech

This approach to free speech fails to recognize something else: a call for genocide, whether by word or symbol, is not the expression of an opinion or one side of a debate. We address this problem next.

Viewpoint Neutrality

We start, as the Court often says, with first principles. Government neutrality toward free speech is sacrosanct. "If there is a bedrock principle underlying the First Amendment, it is that the government may not prohibit the expression of an idea simply because society finds the idea itself offensive or disagreeable,"[9] wrote Justice William J. Brennan in invalidating the Texas law that prohibited burning an American flag. Or, as Justice Robert H. Jackson put it in the 1943 case invalidating West Virginia's mandate that all children must swear allegiance to the American flag:

> If there is any fixed star in our constitutional constellation, it is that no official, high or petty, can prescribe what shall be orthodox in politics, nationalism, religion, or other matters of opinion or force citizens to confess by word or act their faith therein.[10]

There is good reason for this. We don't want the government restricting the content of speech because that would reduce what speech each of us can say, hear, or share in the marketplace of ideas. But it is important to recognize that the government does this anyway, often in ways we generally support—such as with gag orders or prohibiting speech that constitutes treason or sexual harassment or perjury or even the prohibition on making jokes about bombs at TSA checkpoints at the airport. It's okay to withdraw some things from the marketplace of ideas in order to safeguard values that are more important, such as national security or the integrity of the judicial system. These are called content restrictions, and they are permitted only in narrow circumstances.

But worse is when government tries to limit not a whole category of speech but just one side of the debate. This is verboten in part because it's unlikely that the government will ever have a legitimate reason to protect one side of an issue while banning the other side. This is why we don't have loyalty oaths and why both left-wing and right-wing newspapers and news shows exist, regardless of who is in power. And it's why states and cities and universities don't have speech codes that limit hate speech.

As we saw with the *Skokie* and *Brandenburg* cases, in the

view of the Supreme Court over generations, hate speech is merely one side of a debate. Maybe we can call the other side of the debate "love speech." And if hate speech and love speech are just two sides of a debate, then the government does not have the constitutional authority to allow one while punishing the other. The Court said as much in the 1992 *R.A.V.* case in which a minor known only by his initials to protect his privacy was prosecuted for burning a cross on a neighbor's lawn. He was charged with violating this ordinance:

> Whoever places on public or private property a symbol, object, appellation, characterization or graffiti, including, but not limited to, a burning cross or Nazi swastika, which one knows or has reasonable grounds to know arouses anger, alarm or resentment in others on the basis of race, color, creed, religion or gender commits disorderly conduct and shall be guilty of a misdemeanor.[11]

The motivation is plain: St. Paul wanted to prohibit certain kinds of hate speech and hate conduct. But Justice Antonin Scalia, in invalidating the ordinance, said that motivation was precisely what was wrong with it. Under the ordinance, certain words could be used by

> those arguing *in favor* of racial, color, etc., tolerance and equality, but could not be used by those speakers' opponents. . . . St. Paul has no such authority to license one side of a debate to fight freestyle, while requiring the other to follow Marquis of Queensberry rules.

St. Paul cannot withdraw from the marketplace of ideas speech that arouses anger, alarm, or resentment without also withdrawing speech that arouses feelings of warmth and fuzziness. To do so is to engage in what the Court has called viewpoint discrimination—that is, regulations that favor one viewpoint while disfavoring another.

But the Court's reasoning seems wrongheaded for two fundamental reasons. First, it is not at all obvious that burning a cross or calling for genocide is "one side of a debate." It's not "free and fearless reasoning" of the kind Brandeis wanted to protect. It's not even an *idea* that belongs in the marketplace of ideas such as advocacy of lowering the tax rate or allowing assisted suicide. The people who use this form of communication are not really interested in debating ideas. They use it not to invite discussion but to trigger a reaction, one of serious psychological damage and fear in their targets and action in solidarity from their allies. What kind of debate includes a cross burning? What kind of a marketplace of ideas includes a call for genocide?

Second, as the violence surrounding the speech in Charlottesville and the conflicts on college campuses illustrate, hate speech is not the mirror image of "love speech." Even though it looks grammatically symmetrical, saying "we love you, come in!" and saying "we hate you, get out!" don't have the same meaning. One hurts and leads to violence; the other doesn't. The Court's repeated treatment of hate speech—including cross burning—as one side of an argument or debate simply ignores the real violence and pain that hate speech engenders.

We can see the problems more clearly when we look at this under a dignity microscope.

No Dignity in Hate Speech

Fundamentally, what is at stake is the human dignity of the targets of such expression. As we have seen, dignity connotes the essential and inherent worth of every human being. By committing to the principle of human dignity, a society says that every person belongs. Every person has a right to be a member of the society, to participate in its activities, to partake of the benefits of membership, and to be respected as a member. No one should have to claim or argue for their humanity.

And we have also seen that equality is a necessary concomitant of dignity. Because every person is born equal in dignity and rights, everyone has an equal right of membership and partici-pation in a dignity-respecting society. If it were otherwise, some people could say that others' lives don't matter or don't matter as much, or that they are not as welcome or welcome at all in the group. Therein lies genocide. So dignity must entail the equal rights of membership to all.

If we think about speech in dignity terms, it becomes clear that not all speech is created equal. Some speech is inclusive and dignity affirming. Other speech creates boundaries and is dignity denying. To march for equal rights or to proclaim gay pride or to have a Greek festival is to expand the circle of human beings who are accorded dignity and equal respect in a society. It is to welcome and affirm the equal value of each. To unite behind banners of racial hierarchy or to call for genocide is to glorify some human beings at the expense of others. It is to sit in judg-ment of another's worthiness while they fight for their humanity and for their right to be recognized.

This, of course, has implications for how we think about free speech. A society that is committed to respecting, protecting, and fulfilling the equal dignity of all human beings could insist on a marketplace of ideas that recognizes every person's equal worthiness. Such a society can withdraw from the marketplace of "ideas" speech or viewpoints that diminish the humanity of others.

The Supreme Court has already laid the groundwork. In 1942, in the famous case of *Chaplinsky v. New Hampshire*, in which a man was convicted for calling the police "damned fas-cists," the Court said the government could withdraw from the marketplace words that "by their very utterance, inflict injury."[12] These kinds of words, the Court said, "are no essential part of any exposition of ideas, and are of such slight social value as a step to truth that any benefit that may be derived from them is clearly outweighed by the social interest in order and morality."[13]

That is as good a description of dignity-diminishing speech as any.

The *Chaplinsky* Court included in these "proscribable" categories defamation and the "lewd and the obscene." The world has changed since then: we have gone softer on the lewd and the obscene, but we have added child pornography to the list of proscribable or unprotected expression, and of course we continue to withdraw from the marketplace, by punishing the speaker, such speech as perjury, fraud, treason, true threats, and so on. The Supreme Court is constantly choosing which types of speech fall into these categories and which speech is protected because it is harmless and contributes to the marketplace. Surely, the most virulent forms of hate speech, such as swastikas, burning crosses, and calls for genocide, could be seen as forming no essential part of ideas and have little social value. Moreover, these kinds of expression cause real dignity harms that the Court should be sensitive to. This is what other countries do, including countries that, like ours, are committed to the principle of freedom of speech both as an individual right and a social and political necessity of a functioning democracy.

Lessons from Abroad

Many countries committed to freedom of speech in principle have nonetheless managed to draw lines that exclude from their marketplace certain virulent forms of hate speech. This is often done in the name of protecting the dignity of those who are the targets of hate speech.

Canada has restricted freedom of speech where people have engaged in racist speech and Holocaust denial.[14] The Canadian criminal code subjects to prison any person who "communicates statements in any public place, incites hatred against any identifiable group where such incitement is likely to lead to a breach of the peace" and any person who "by communicating statements, other than in private conversation, wilfully promotes hatred against any identifiable group."[15] But even here, to the extent that the concern is about breaches of the peace, it does not address the real dignity harms.

The German criminal code is more direct. It prohibits the "incitement of masses," which it defines in part as violating "the human dignity of others by insulting, maliciously maligning or defaming" a "national, racial, religious group or a group defined by their ethnic origin" on account of "their belonging to one of the aforementioned groups or sections of the population."[16] In one subsection specifically prohibiting Holocaust denial, the law establishes that "whoever publicly or in a meeting disturbs the public peace in a manner which violates the dignity of the victims by approving of, glorifying or justifying National Socialist tyranny and arbitrary rule incurs a penalty of imprisonment for a term not exceeding three years or a fine."[17] Glorifying the ideology of hate and inhumanity is an insult to a person's humanity and a harm to their dignity, which the German government is obligated to protect under Article 1.

Brazil prohibits "the practice of racism" directly in its 1988 Constitution, establishing it to be "a non-bailable crime, with no limitation, subject to the penalty of confinement."[18] This provision has been held to apply not only to racist speech but to anti-LGBTQ+ speech as well.[19]

These and other nations like them have a strong commitment to democratic values and freedom of speech. They are also all committed to protecting human dignity as a matter of constitutional right and fundamental values. Thus, the limitations are based, in one way or another, on the need to protect the dignity of people who are especially vulnerable by virtue of their membership in certain groups. These provisions would likely have subjected to punishment people who incite public hatred under the banner of uniting the right or who called for the genocide of any group.

A Free-Speech Regime That Protects Human Dignity

Justice Brandeis's opinion in *Whitney* is not only a manifesto for free speech but also a manifesto for a free people. Indeed, it is the closest the Supreme Court has come to connecting the dots of the Constitution from individual freedom to democratic governance through human dignity. As Brandeis explained:

> Those who won our independence believed that the final end of the State was to make men free to develop their faculties, and that, in its government, the deliberative forces should prevail over the arbitrary. They valued liberty both as an end, and as a means.[20]

This language translates directly into so much of today's discourse about human dignity. As we have seen in previous chapters, the idea of dignity is most often associated with the full and free development of the personality and with the control and agency people want to have over their own lives. These values sound in human dignity not only because they derive from the "reason and conscience" with which all human beings are endowed (as the UDHR pronounces in Article I) and not only because they are the inherent goods of the human spirit but also because they are the basis of a free and deliberative government. Dignity, like liberty, is both an ends and a means. We respect the dignity of all to have a society in which all can live with dignity.

These principles can be applied to the regulation of freedom of speech. Yes, speech should be as free as possible, to ensure that as many people as possible can share and have access to as many ideas as possible, so that they can choose for themselves which ideas they like and which ones they reject. This is what

Justice Brandeis was arguing for and what Justice Oliver Wendell Holmes meant when, in 1919, he advocated for an unregulated marketplace of ideas. This is why the Supreme Court in the landmark defamation case, *New York Times Co. v. Sullivan,* said that the marketplace should be "uninhibited, robust, and wide open."[21] And this is how Justice Harlan put it, in upholding the right of a young man in 1972 to wear a jacket with the words "Fuck the Draft" embroidered on it:

> The constitutional right of free expression is powerful medicine in a society as diverse and populous as ours. It is designed and intended to remove governmental restraints from the arena of public discussion, putting the decision as to what views shall be voiced largely into the hands of each of us, in the hope that use of such freedom will ultimately produce a more capable citizenry and more perfect polity and in the belief that no other approach would comport with the premise of individual dignity and choice upon which our political system rests.[22]

But of course, there are limits. Justice Holmes recognized this too, when he said that, notwithstanding an open marketplace, a person could be punished for falsely shouting "fire" in a crowded theater and causing a panic. Indeed, limitations on speech are, in our society, all around us, from trademark infringement to treason. These limits are justified where the interest in free speech is subordinated to other interests deemed more important—such as intellectual property rights, economic rights, reputational interests, or structural interests like the interests of national security or the integrity of the courts. These restrictions are allowed both because the speech does not constitute an "idea" and because it causes discernible harm. Couldn't the same be said of the most dignity-denying forms of "hate speech"?

FIVE

How to Find Dignity in the
Criminal Legal System

A Legal System or a Justice System?

Consider these facts: Of all the prisoners everywhere in the world, one-fifth are incarcerated in the United States. The thirty-six jurisdictions that have the highest incarceration rates on earth are all US states. Blacks are incarcerated at nearly five times the rate of whites in America; the death row population is divided equally between blacks and whites.

The United States is the only country other than Somalia that has not ratified the international Convention on the Rights of the Child. The United States tries children as adults, sentences children to live their entire lives and to die in prison with adults. The use of solitary confinement—sometimes for terms that exceed what the international community defines as torture when applied to adults—is widespread for youth in prisons and jails in the United States.

More than half the women who are incarcerated have not been convicted of any crime; they are awaiting trial, incarcerated most often because they cannot afford bail. It is estimated that approximately 85 percent of women in prison were sexually abused before they arrived in prison and are three times more likely than men to be sexually abused by prison or jail staff.

The dignity violations don't end upon release. Although the numbers seem to be dropping, nearly four million adults in America live under "community supervision"—that is, they are on probation or parole and their lives are supervised by correctional officers.[1] If they formed their own community, it would have the population of Oklahoma, and they would be entitled to five representatives and two senators in Congress. But voting rights are typically withdrawn from people who are incarcerated and for many who have been released. Although African Americans make up about 14 percent of the US population overall, they make up about 30 percent of the population living under supervision:[2] that is, with their autonomy and dignity compromised. And according to the National Conference of State Legislatures, "On any given day, around 280,000 people are in prison for violating a condition of probation or parole. This is nearly 25% of the total prison population" in the United States.[3]

For far too many people, the American criminal justice system is not just at all. And for all Americans, it is a drain on the economy: we spend about $265 billion annually on federal, state, and local corrections and the entire police and court systems.[4] According to the center-right American Action Forum, "The societal costs of incarceration—lost earnings, adverse health effects, and the damage to the families of the incarcerated—are estimated at up to three times the direct costs, bringing the total burden of our criminal justice system to $1.2 trillion." And for what? The American Action Forum continues: "The outcomes of this expense are only a marginal reduction in crime, reduced earnings for the convicted, and a high likelihood of formerly incarcerated individuals returning to prison."[5]

But this is not like other areas of law and policy, which pose wicked problems because of their complexity or because of the conflicting values they implicate. Mass incarceration (shorthand for our criminal legal system) violates human dignity in numerous profound and quotidian ways that could be alleviated or remedied without any cost to society and, in fact, with financial and social benefits to society. This is the point that is too often lost in the American conversation about crime: we can be safe *and* respect the dignity of all persons. It does not have to be a zero-sum game.

So what would a criminal legal system look like if it respected the human dignity of all? What would it look like if it were a true criminal *justice* system?

Nothing Less than the Dignity of Man

There are sprinkles of dignity throughout the American legal system. The Supreme Court has repeatedly held that the Eighth Amendment—prohibiting cruel and unusual punishment—is "about nothing less than the dignity of man."[6] It has said that "prisoners retain the essence of human dignity inherent in all persons. Respect for that dignity animates the Eighth Amendment prohibition against cruel and unusual punishment."[7]

Judge Neomi Rao of the US Circuit Court for the DC Circuit (appointed by Donald Trump) has written about the importance of dignity not only in our constitutional law but in how we construct our society, how we define ourselves, and what we value:

> Dignity in constitutional law and political life cannot simply be brushed aside. In modern constitutional systems, dignity is already a preeminent value. Even in the United States, it is increasingly a part of our discourse in thinking about individual rights and government action.[8]

Judge Rao continues by making the normative argument to spur law reform to better protect human dignity:

> So it makes sense to think about what conceptions of dignity we want to promote in our political and social community. The type of dignity that a society protects is part of how a community defines itself—how individuals belong to the community and how the state must act to respect human dignity. An appeal to dignity cannot solve conflicts between competing visions of the good life, but it gives us an opportunity to discuss what we value and why.[9]

Judge Thomas Ambro (appointed by Bill Clinton and sitting by designation in the District of Delaware) wrote in a prisoner rights case in 2023: "Dignity, or respect of our fellow human beings, is an important principle underlying many constitutional rights. Because of this, the Supreme Court has routinely discussed dignity in cases where plaintiffs seek to vindicate those rights."[10] Judge Ambro cited a series of cases in support of the claim that dignity is prevalent in US constitutional law, involving freedom of speech, privacy, and criminal rights, including the right against self-incrimination. Indeed, the reason we give *Miranda* warnings is precisely that "the constitutional foundation underlying the privilege [against self-incrimination] is the respect a government—state or federal—must accord to the dignity and integrity of its citizens."[11]

Nonetheless, American jurists have rarely, if ever, described what they mean by dignity in the context of the criminal legal system. This is a shame both because rights are precarious if they are not fully explicated and because a fuller understanding of how certain rights are necessary in order to protect human dignity would enhance judicial and social commitment to those rights. This is particularly important in the context of the criminal law that is already used to deprive people of rights. Dignity rights stand apart: they are inviolable because they are rooted not in the Constitution or what a court says the Constitution is but in the human person. If we pay attention to human dignity, we can start to get a sense of what we want our criminal legal system to look like.

This chapter reimagines the criminal legal system through a dignity lens, focusing on three nodes in the criminal justice time line: first encounters with police on the streets, sentencing, and conditions of incarceration.[12] The survey is necessarily brief and a summary but will provide insight into how we should respect human dignity throughout the legal system.

Arrest: Police Brutality and Training

We all know the names of people who were killed by police while driving to work, lying in bed, walking across the street, getting ice cream, and so on. In 2009, 84 people were shot by police;[13] in 2023, there were 1,191 victims of police violence.[14] In 2023, there were fourteen days in which police did *not* kill a person.[15] This does not count violence by police against people that did not result in death. There is no evidence that violence by police makes neighborhoods safer.

The movement that emerged in the wake of the 2020 killing of George Floyd that advocated to "defund the police" galvanized an important conversation. It got a bad rap because, taken to its extreme, it would mean the end of police enforcement of our laws, which most of us don't want, including those of us who live in crime-ridden neighborhoods and in communities that are most likely to be adversely targeted by police. Most of us want some kind of police system. And we want a police force that treats people with dignity and a system that cares for the mental and physical well-being of all individuals, even as it seeks to enforce the law. The real meaning of "defund the police" was, therefore, never to remove all funding from police forces but to shift funding from the use of force against vulnerable people to programs that would make people less vulnerable and help those who are. For the sloganeers, the slogan means

> divesting from institutions that kill, harm, cage and control our communities, and investing in violence prevention and interruption, housing, health care, income support, employment, and other community-based safety strategies that will produce safer communities for everyone.[16]

This is fundamentally a dignity-based approach. It does not seek divestment from all aspects of policing, only those that involve dehumanization and brutality; this, along with better police training practices, would help ensure that all people are treated with dignity and respect. It seeks to increase resources in social systems that ensure that all people have housing, health care, income, and safe communities so that everybody can live with dignity. Living with dignity in safety and with the respect of others, including law enforcement, will help ensure that every person can fully develop their personalities, and this in turn will reduce crime, which would, one hopes, reduce incarceration rates and reinforce full personhood. This way, the cycle of criminality and incarceration turns into a cycle of dignity.

Sentencing: Why Do We Lock People Up?

In the United States, we sentence more people for more time than in any other country on earth. Although many people believe that incarceration under any circumstances is inconsistent with human dignity, we don't need to abolish all prisons to have a criminal legal system that respects human dignity. We just need to think about why we sentence people to prison; that is, what are we hoping to accomplish by forcing people to spend the most precious thing they have—time—behind bars? And what is the appropriate length of a stay in prison needed to accomplish the social purpose of holding someone accountable for committing a crime?

So why do we lock people up? First, about half a million people are languishing in our nation's prisons and jails without having been convicted of any crime.[17] They are in pretrial detention, meaning, shockingly, that they have been deprived of their liberty for reasons other than a finding of guilt—notwithstanding the presumption of innocence that defines a legal system under a just rule of law. A half million people is about the entire population of Kansas City, Missouri. Pretrial detainees encompass approximately 60 percent of the incarcerated population,[18] and they make up more than 70 percent of the jail population.[19] Most of these individuals are incarcerated because they cannot afford to post bail:[20] of those accused of felonies, almost 90 percent cannot afford to make bail,[21] making up 38 percent of people who are living in jail while awaiting trial. Three-quarters of the people in jail without convictions have only been charged with low-level drug or property crimes or other nonviolent crimes.[22] Those are the people we are locking up. They are imprisoned for no particular reason except poverty and misfortune. In a society committed to human dignity—or even a society committed to due process and the rule of law—there should not be pretrial detention except under the most egregious circumstances. And this doesn't even count the people who are resentenced to prison for violations of probation and parole, who make up about 42 percent of prison admissions each day.[23]

For those who have been convicted of a crime, there are reasons why we take away their liberty. The Supreme Court has recognized four penological goals—retribution (punishment), deterrence, incapacitation, and rehabilitation.[24]

Retribution is "punishment imposed (as on a convicted criminal) for purposes of repayment or revenge for the wrong committed."[25] Many countries have eschewed retribution as a valid purpose of the criminal justice system because it violates human dignity: it objectifies people by putting them behind bars in order to achieve a social goal (punishment). Using them as a means to an end violates basic principles of human dignity.

Retribution is additionally incompatible with human dignity because it contains no limiting principle or even articulable goal: How much punishment is enough? Where is the line that distinguishes proportionate punishment from excessive punishment? Often, in the popular vernacular, retribution is renamed as "justice," for example, when people call for harsh punishments in order to have "justice" for the victims. But incarceration does not right the wrong or balance the scales of justice; it simply harms the dignity of the person convicted.

Deterrence punishes a person to teach a lesson to themselves or to others to make it less likely that they or others will commit the same or a similar crime in the future.[26] Deterrence is additionally problematic because the evidence about the effectiveness of imprisonment as a deterrent is uncertain at best. According to the National Institute of Justice,

> Sending an individual convicted of a crime to prison isn't a very effective way to deter crime. Prisons are good for punishing criminals and keeping them off the street, but prison sentences (particularly long sentences) are unlikely to deter future crime. Prisons actually may have the opposite effect: Inmates learn more effective crime strategies from each other, and time spent in prison may desensitize many to the threat of future imprisonment.

Moreover, "increasing the severity of punishment does little to deter crime. Laws and policies designed to deter crime by focusing mainly on increasing the severity of punishment are ineffective partly because criminals know little about the sanctions for specific crimes. More severe punishments do not 'chasten' individuals convicted of crimes, and prisons may exacerbate recidivism."[27] The Supreme Court acknowledges this in *Gregg v. Georgia* regarding capital punishment: "Statistical attempts to evaluate the worth of the death penalty as a deterrent to crimes by potential offenders have occasioned a great deal of debate. The results simply have been inconclusive."[28]

Incapacitation simply removes someone from society or restricts their liberty in order to prevent them from committing a crime in the future.[29] Incapacitation may be a valid public policy insofar as it is necessary to incapacitate a person in order to ensure the safety of the community. But it is problematic from a dignity standpoint because it imposes a punishment not for what the person has done but for what they could (but may not) do next. It therefore imposes a punishment on the basis of presumed future guilt, not on the basis of the person's actual conduct. This violates the dignity-based principle of presumed innocence and responsibility. The level of certainty that incapacity is necessary to prevent future criminal conduct must be very, very high in order to adhere to the standards of dignity.

Rehabilitation (sometimes called reintegration or socialization) is the only goal that is consonant with dignity because it is "the process of restoring someone to a useful and constructive place in society."[30] It therefore takes dignity as its purpose and its means: by treating everyone with dignity, the state makes it more likely that the person can live with dignity and reduces the likelihood that they will engage in harmful criminal activity in the future.

Following this principle, the Canadian Supreme Court has written:

> The objective of rehabilitation is intimately linked to human dignity in that it reflects the conviction that all individuals carry within themselves the capacity to reform and re-enter society. . . . [The] criminal law is based, and must be based, "on a conception of the human being as an agent who is free and autonomous and, as a result, capable of change."[31]

Retribution, deterrence, and incapacitation, by contrast, mark a person's character by defining them according to their action and assuming that a person who has committed a crime in the past will do so again.

According to an extensive study conducted by the Vera Institute, sentencing in Germany and the Netherlands is limited to rehabilitation as understood in the sense of resocialization.[32] Indeed, rehabilitation is clearly stated in the law:

> According to Germany's Prison Act, the sole aim of incarceration is to enable prisoners to lead a life of social responsibility free of crime upon release, requiring that prison life be as similar as possible to life in the community (sometimes referred to as "the principle of normalization") and organized in such a way as to facilitate reintegration into society.[33]

Similarly, the core aim of the Netherlands 1998 Penitentiary Principles Act is the "re-socialization of prisoners in which incarceration is carried out with as few restrictions as possible through the principle of association (both within prison and between prisoners and the community), and not separation." Thus, "prisoners are encouraged to maintain and cultivate relationships with others both within and outside the prison walls."[34]

Understanding rehabilitation as reintegration or resocialization is the best way to ensure that the goals of incarceration align with human dignity. As we have seen, an essential component of dignity is ensuring each person is able to fully develop their personality in community with others.

Because sentencing practices in both Germany and the Netherlands focus more on rehabilitation than retribution, intermediate and noncustodial sanctions are used more frequently, with incarceration used only sparingly and for much shorter periods of time than in the United States.[35] Using incarceration only when no alternative is suitable ensures that more people can maintain greater connections with their communities while they are paying their debt to society.[36] This respects their dignity as people while the sentence is served and contributes to their well-being and reconnection with society upon completion of the sentence.

Another consideration that a dignity-based criminal justice system needs to consider is the length of sentences. Again, the United States is an outlier among democratic nations in the length of sentences, the use of life sentences (with or without parole), and the application of long sentences and life sentences to minors.

Beginning in the 1970s, the criminal legal system shifted away from indeterminate sentencing and rehabilitation to focus more on crime control to be achieved through incapacitation and retribution.[37] This trend emphasized punishment and clearly established terms, known as mandatory minimum sentencing, that withdraw a judge's discretion to impose a more lenient sentence, regardless of individual circumstances.[38] In the 1990s, sentences became even harsher, with the advent of the "three-strikes" laws, which require that a person be sentenced to life after a third serious offense, with "seriousness" varying widely across different jurisdictions.[39] Unique in the world, the three-strikes laws exemplify the total rejection of any rehabilitative or resocializing inclination and, with it, the disposal of human dignity: without regard to individual circumstances, the nature of past convictions, or the likelihood of effective reentry, three-strikes laws impact the core of a person's dignity by reducing the value of their life to a simple and harsh rule. This, combined with the advent of truth in sentencing laws, which require that a sentenced person complete a minimum of 85 percent of their sentence before they can be considered for release, has led to harsher sentencing, longer sentences being served, and less judicial discretion in sentencing[40]—all in violation of principles of human dignity, which value the inherent and inalienable right of each person to live their entire life with dignity and the need to treat each person as a unique individual.

While these policies have not contributed to a reduction in crime, they have dramatically increased the prison population. The Vera Institute reports that by 2012, the impact of these policies

> had become clear: in 40 years, the prison population grew by 705 percent, from nearly 175,000 state inmates in 1972 to just under 1.4 million as of January 1, 2012. With more than one in every 104 American adults in prison or jail, the U.S. has the highest incarceration rate in the world—at 716 per 100,000 residents.[41]

By contrast, the number of residents incarcerated per one hundred thousand is seventy-nine in Germany and eighty-two in the Netherlands.[42]

Incarceration—with Dignity?

Much has been written about the deplorable conditions of incarceration in American prisons and jails, whether publicly or privately run. Suffice it to say that in most situations, dignity is simply nonexistent inside prison walls. The reasons are manifold and include the lack of binding obligations to respect dignity and the reliance on self-reporting under such schemes as the Prison Rape Elimination Act,[43] the lack of training and the institutional incentives to avoid respecting human dignity, the costs of maintaining clean and healthful facilities, the increasing mental and physical health needs of prisoners, societal racism and sexism and other forms of discrimination that are exacerbated inside prisons, and so on. All of this is unrestricted and compounded by the near-absolute policy of deference given to prison facilities by the courts, which diminishes accountability for abuse by prison staff—even in a system that is meant to be all about holding people accountable for their wrongdoings.

Some organizations have begun to explore what a dignity-respecting carceral system would look like. The Vera Institute for Justice, for instance, has developed a multipronged program called "Dignity behind Bars."[44] But courts have been reluctant to impose obligations on government officials to ensure that people inside are treated with dignity.

Montana furnishes one counterexample as the only state whose Constitution guarantees an actionable right to dignity. (Puerto Rico's Constitution also does.) In *Walker v. State*, the Montana Supreme Court considered the case of a person who was already in an especially vulnerable state. Walker suffered from a host of mental health issues that made him especially vulnerable because he was dependent on others for his care and was susceptible to enormous suffering if not appropriately cared for. Yet Walker was subject to particularly horrific conditions, the details of which are hard to read.

> Walker asserted that the living conditions in A-block were intolerable. Numerous inmates who resided in A-block testified about the filthy, uninhabitable cells. These inmates testified that the cells commonly had blood, feces, vomit and other types of debris in the cells they were forced to inhabit. One inmate recounted an instance where he was placed in a cell with human waste rubbed all over the walls and vomit in the corner. He claims the corrections staff ignored his complaints and told him to "live with it." Another inmate testified that he had bloodied a cell by smashing his head against the wall. His blood remained in the cell until Walker eventually inhabited the cell. After Walker was removed from that cell sometime later, the inmate who originally bloodied the cell was moved back in. He testified that the blood streaks and the words he previously had written in blood on the wall of the cell remained unchanged.[45]

This is how we treat people in America. Thankfully, the Montana Supreme Court insisted on better living conditions for people in Walker's situation. The constitutional provision on which the court relied reads as follows:

Section 4.   Individual dignity. The dignity of the human being is inviolable. No person shall be denied the equal protection of the laws. Neither the state nor any person, firm, corporation, or institution shall discriminate against any person in the exercise of his civil or political rights on account of race, color, sex, culture, social origin or condition, or political or religious ideas.[46]

The court held that Walker's dignity rights were violated, and it identified an affirmative obligation on the state to take measures necessary to protect the dignity of every person within its care.

Without a dignity provision in the constitution, it's much harder—though perhaps not impossible—to get a court to pay attention to the dignity rights of people who are incarcerated. In 2023, a Third Circuit judge sitting by designation in the District of Delaware held that the plaintiffs—all of whom were incarcerated and claiming numerous instances of excessive use of force by prison staff could not bring an independent claim that their dignity was violated; nonetheless, it held that "although these claims for violating dignity are not independently recognized, Plaintiffs may proceed with other claims, such as those for Eighth and Fourteenth Amendment violations, that seek to remedy the same underlying violations of their dignity."[47] This is an opening for advocates to pursue.

True Justice

Having a criminal legal system that respects human dignity is not complicated. It simply requires attending to the dignity needs of every person in society, including victims of crime and including those who are suspected of criminal activity and those who are convicted of crimes and sentenced to prison. When we have a system that keeps society safe from excessive criminal activity and still respects the dignity of those who are system implicated, we can call it a true criminal *justice* system.

SIX

The Injustices, Inequalities, and Indignities of Poverty

Two Seeds in One Pod

Dignity contains two seeds in one pod. The first is a justice seed, the seed that ensures that every person can live with dignity and is treated with dignity. This is the part of the story that emphasizes dignity's universality, that all people at all times and in all places should be treated "as a person," just by virtue of having been born a "member of the human family," as the Universal Declaration of Human Rights says. For our purposes, this means that every person is entitled to a certain quality of life, particularly in a country as wealthy and as industrially advanced as ours. Abject poverty, homelessness, forcing people to choose between paying rent and paying for food are all injustices that violate human dignity because they demean the quality of human life and degrade the human spirit.

The other seed relates to equality or, more specifically, to equity.[1] The UDHR tells us that every member of the human family "is born equal in dignity and rights." In other words, at birth, we all have the same fundamental value and the same rights to the opportunity to live with dignity. The inequities we see all around us are social constructions that result in some people being able to live in peace, privacy, and security and to fully develop their personalities and pursue their dreams, while others are vulnerable to all kinds of suffering and struggle to get through the day. As Matthew McManus says, "Where individuals enjoy less dignity, it is the consequence of inadequate and even hostile acts or omissions by social institutions that have a responsibility to care for them."[2] We create these inequities.

In the United States, we have both problems: far too much poverty overall as well as vast inequalities of wealth. A dignity-based vision of economic justice would respond to both problems. It would ensure a safety net and would ensure that everyone is treated equitably.

We should remember a few things at the outset. First, this society has never existed in America. We are not fixing a working system that somehow got a bug in it and broke down. A dignity-based economic system has to be invented from scratch. Second, that is by design. To promote a dignity-based economic system is to counter centuries of policies designed to ensure that some people can profit but not designed to ensure that every person can live with dignity. And to change a system at its roots takes courage, as Justice Brandeis said in his 1927 opinion in the *Whitney* case.

Third, these inequalities and injustices result not as much from an economic ordering as from our government system. That is, poverty and inequality exist not as a result of myriad economic decisions made by unnamed and unaccountable actors or by some invisible hand that is impossible to control. No, they exist in America because of political decisions we make every day and, especially, once every four years. Our government chooses how much of a safety net to provide for people so they have health care and shelter. It chooses whether, or not, to provide food vouchers so that children don't go hungry. It chooses whether to regulate businesses to ensure that all employees have safe working conditions and adequate time off, and it chooses how much to enforce those regulations. Judges decide whether to hold government actors to account for failing to protect the dignity of every person. These are political choices we make about what kind of society we want, whether we want American society to protect the dignity of all, or not.

Ultimately, these are decisions about what we the people want from our government. In the United States, the answer tends to be very little. In other countries and regions of the world, by contrast, people are much more likely to look to the government to help solve their problems, not just in emergencies but day to day. And in many of those countries, courts play important roles in ensuring that the government acts to enable every person to live with dignity—with equity and justice.

This chapter briefly surveys indications of poverty in America and shows how various aspects of poverty (lack of shelter, inaccessible education, inadequate health care) are all interrelated and interdependent and all connected to human dignity. It also shows how government policies affect both injustice and inequities and how courts can alleviate the indignities of poverty by learning from their counterparts in other countries.

Poverty and Dignity

I once heard a story about a woman who was living in her car with her kids. A few months earlier, she had been living in a decent apartment and had a job that paid the rent and her basic expenses. But one day, on her way to work, she tripped on a sidewalk curb and twisted her ankle badly. Because she could not walk, she was unable to get to work on time, and after a few days of not being able to walk or drive to work, she was fired, losing not only her job but also the means to pay for her medical care and her rent. And there she was in her car, which she couldn't drive but she could sleep in with her children, with no prospects. In America, you step off the sidewalk and fall through the cracks; there is no safety net. Sure, she still had her inherent human dignity. But how dignified did she feel reading a bedtime story to her kids as she tucked them into the back seat, relieved that, this night, they weren't too hungry to fall asleep and didn't ask too many questions about when they would go back home or what they should tell their friends?

One thing is for sure: this woman is not alone. In 2022, "37.9 million people lived in poverty," which accounts for 12.4 percent of Americans, including about the same percentage of children (having more than doubled from 5.4 percent in 2021).[3] It's as if nearly the entire population—every single person—in California or the combined population of Texas and Arizona—all lived below the poverty line.

And keep in mind that living above the poverty line does not mean you don't struggle. The measures of poverty used in the United States fall far short of what it means to live with dignity. "The U.S. poverty level is now $13,590 for individuals and $23,030 for a family of three."[4] And her children are not alone: the Children's Defense Fund estimates that "*11 million children live in poverty, including 1 in 7 children of color and 1 in 6 children under 5.*"[5] This is an injustice of monumental proportions. People should not live on the streets, in their cars, or in shelters. Kids should not go to sleep, and wake up, hungry. Today, the United States ranks 28 out of 38 countries in the Organization for Economic Cooperation and Development in poverty rates,[6] and "of the 38 countries in the [OECD], only four are more unequal: Chile, Costa Rica, Mexico and Turkey."[7]

While it is difficult to analyze economic inequality—largely because so many different factors contribute to differences in income and wealth—the consensus seems to be that American society in the last few decades is becoming less equal. According to Minneapolis Federal Monetary Bank adviser Jonathan Heathcote, "The general notion that inequality is widening is broadly correct."[8]

This is true not just in America but around the world.[9] According to the *World Inequality Report*, "The poorest half of the global population barely owns any wealth at all, possessing just 2% of the total. In contrast, the richest 10% of the global population own 76% of all wealth. On average, the poorest half of the population owns $4,100 per adult and the top 10% own $771,300 on average."[10] The *World Inequality Report* makes a few other important points. First, inequality is increasing: "Income and wealth inequalities have been on the rise nearly everywhere since the 1980s, following a series of deregulation and liberalization programs." Second, the rise in inequality has not been uniform: "Certain countries have experienced spectacular increases in inequality (including the US, Russia and India) while others (European countries and China) have experienced relatively smaller rises." And third, the report concludes that "these differences . . . confirm that inequality is not inevitable, it is a political choice."[11]

Of course, people who live in poverty still have inherent dignity, as much as anyone else. But imagine how hard it would be to live with dignity if you're chronically hungry, or worried about whether you'll pay the electricity bill or buy your kid shoes that fit, or if you go to the emergency room for basic health care and ignore dental problems because you can't afford to fix them, or if you're always worried about how to keep yourself or your kids safe because of the gun violence in your neighborhood. Imagine the toll that takes on your sense of your own self-worth, your ability to plan your life; imagine how that limits your ability to fully develop your personality and to help your children develop theirs.

The comprehensive assault on dignity occurs because poverty is not a single thing; it is a concatenation of problems that compound one another. In international law, we refer to this as the indivisibility of rights—the notion that rights are interconnected and that the denial of one right impacts the ability to enjoy others. The lack of money to buy nutritious food or to live in a decent home makes one vulnerable to crime and more likely to have illness (from lead in the pipes, mold in the walls, stress), which affects a person's bodily integrity and ability to work or learn effectively. This limits their ability to develop themselves fully and impedes their ability to engage with others in their community on the basis of equality. These are not just problems; they are assaults on human dignity. So when we focus on how people can live with dignity, we need to think about the many mutually reinforcing ways that dignity is threatened and compromised.

The dignity implications of poverty are not hard to see. If we think of dignity as implicating the various principles of personhood, humanity, and decency described in Chapter 1, we can see that poverty, for both children and adults, impacts almost all the values we associate with dignity: fully developing one's personality, having agency over how one lives one's life in accordance with the personhood principle; living free of humiliation and being seen as a person in one's full humanity in the eyes of others; and living decently with protection from elements and adequate nutrition and sanitation.

The important thing to recognize here is that imposing these burdens on 12 percent of our population, including eleven million children, is not natural or inevitable and it is certainly not desirable. It is a political choice we make individually and collectively to ignore our common humanity.

Poverty and Government

If we are all born equal in dignity and rights, it's what happens after birth that renders us unequal. Society's ordering of people, through laws and culture, puts some people in positions of power and control over others and keeps others in positions of persistent subordination and vulnerability. Our laws determine whether there is a safety net for someone who trips on a curb and sets that safety net at a certain level—high enough so she doesn't starve, or higher still so she can live in an apartment and get decent medical care, or higher still so that her kids can get a good education and fully develop their personalities through high school or college. Our government makes decisions every day about how much to protect people from the indignities of poverty and how much to assuage the indignities that occur.

In a detailed and comprehensive analysis of poverty in the United States, Mark Rank and Tom Hirschl conclude that the reasons for the discrepancy between the United States and the rest of the industrialized world are twofold.

> First, the social safety net in the United States is much weaker than in virtually every other country [in the OECD]. Second, the United States has been plagued by relatively low wages at the bottom of the income distribution scale when compared to other developed countries. These factors combine to contribute to both the relative and absolute depths of U.S. poverty in comparison to other industrialized nations.[12]

Both of these are political choices. We choose whether we want to give people a safety net and whether we want it to raise them out of misery, out of poverty, or to a life of dignity. And even wage stagnation, which is invariably described in the passive voice ("wages have stagnated") as if it's some impersonal and indomitable force that has crushed lower wages down into the ground, when in fact this too is a product of political decisions to raise the minimum wage, to enhance job security, and to protect workers' quality of life beyond wage earnings—or not.

Here is one clear example of how our government chooses whether people will live in poverty or not. Childhood poverty is a significant problem whether looked at domestically or internationally. On their website, Confronting Poverty, Rank and Hirschl report that "the United States has the highest standards of living at the middle and upper ends of the income distribution scale, yet for children at the lower end, their standards of living fall behind most other industrialized nations."[13] The government has not been unconcerned about this. The Child Tax Credit (CTC), for instance, "helps families with qualifying children get a tax break,"[14] according to the Internal Revenue Service. It does so by providing a credit or refund on taxes paid; this means that it provides no benefit to people who are so poor that they do not pay taxes. Nonetheless, it was effective in "alleviating some of the burdens on low-income earners and single-headed households. Prior to the Covid pandemic, the CTC was responsible for lifting over four million children out of poverty through various governmentally accessible programs in 2018. [Parents] reported spending their monthly CTC payments on household necessities like food, rent, and clothing."[15]

In 2021, during COVID, Congress temporarily extended the CTC to more poor families. The result was immediate: childhood poverty plummeted to 5.2 percent, the lowest on record. According to *Time* magazine, in 2021 America had "experienced tremendous improvements in poverty reduction. . . . Safety net programs including expanded child tax credit lifted millions out of poverty and provided direct aid to low-income households."[16] But the benefits to children did not last because in 2022, Congress allowed the expansion to expire and the CTC reverted to the more limited benefit of the pre-COVID years. *Time* reported, "As programs like this were allowed to expire, the data shows that those programs were a short-lived lifeline." Again, the result was immediate: childhood poverty jumped to "12.4 percent in 2022, erasing all of the record gains made against child poverty over the previous two years. Progress made in 2021 in narrowing the glaring differences between the poverty rates of Black and Latino children compared to white children was largely reversed."[17]

The nonpartisan Center for Budget and Policy Priorities estimates that "some 19 million children live in families whose incomes are too low to qualify for the full credit. This includes nearly half (46 percent) of Black children, 1 in 3 Latino and American Indian and Alaska Native children, about 1 in 6 white and 1 in 7 Asian children, and 1 in 3 children in rural counties."[18] It concludes that "renewing this 2021 credit would have kept about 3 million children above the poverty line in 2022—including 975,000 white children, 603,000 Black children, 988,000 Latino children, and 57,000 Asian children—avoiding *more than half* of the actual jump in the child poverty rate." The link between cause and effect is evident: "Today's stunning rise in poverty is the direct result of policy choices—including Congress's decision to allow the successful Child Tax Credit expansion to expire."[19]

The point here is twofold: first, we know how to bring people, including children, out of poverty; and, second, Americans elect people to represent them in Washington who choose not to do the thing that will bring people, including children, out of poverty. That is, we choose representatives in Congress who deny children the right to live with dignity. There is no benefit to them or to us to have so many children living below the poverty line, but we elect those people anyway, and they vote against children anyway.

The reasons for these results are far beyond the scope of this book. Maybe we don't ask enough of our government. Maybe we don't trust government officials or the Civil Service. Maybe there is something in the American character that makes us more concerned about ourselves—that vaunted rugged individualism—and less inclined to help others on a social scale. Maybe we are too committed to the myth that there is an even economic playing field and that success and failure in the market result only from hard work and skill, as if we were all playing a Monopoly game in which everyone starts out with the same chance of success.[20] Racism and xenophobia undoubtedly also play a role.[21] Whatever the reason or reasons, it is beyond dispute that we have extensive poverty in the United States, including extensive childhood poverty; that we choose to ignore the indignities of poverty, including the indignities to millions of children; and that we could choose a different course.

Economic Justice and the Courts

Poverty is a political problem, and it largely requires political solution. Our Constitution does not specifically impose any particular economic order on the country, it does not mandate what the poverty rate should be, and it does not insist that our government care about the extremely poor in our society. So our courts have never insisted on economic policies that would alleviate poverty or that would ensure access to health care, or a quality education, or access to food, indoor plumbing, or a healthy environment. But the obligation is there nonetheless, both as a matter of human dignity and as a matter of international law.

International law recognizes that the right to live is the right to live with dignity.[22] Interpreting the right to life guaranteed in the International Covenant of Civil and Political Rights (to which the United States is a party), the United Nations Human Rights Council has explained that the right to life "should not be interpreted narrowly."[23]

The duty to protect life also implies that States parties should take appropriate measures to address the general conditions in society that may give rise to direct threats to life or prevent individuals from enjoying their right to life with dignity. . . .

These general conditions may include high levels of criminal and gun violence, pervasive traffic and industrial accidents, degradation of the environment, deprivation of indigenous peoples' land, territories and resources, the prevalence of life-threatening diseases, extensive substance abuse, widespread hunger and malnutrition and extreme poverty and homelessness.[24]

This imposes on governments, including the United States, the obligation not just to avoid imposing indignities on people but to take affirmative measures to alleviate the indignities that people endure. The Human Rights Council further indicated some actions that states should take.

The measures called for to address adequate conditions for protecting the right to life include, where necessary, measures designed to ensure access without delay by individuals to essential goods and services such as food, water, shelter, health care, electricity and sanitation, and other measures designed to promote and facilitate adequate general conditions, such as the bolstering of effective emergency health services, emergency response operations (including firefighters, ambulance services and police forces) and social housing programmes. States parties should also develop strategic plans for advancing the enjoyment of the right to life.[25]

Courts in some countries have followed suit and held their governments to account. While they rarely get into the details of what is, specifically, required to ensure that every person can live with dignity, some courts have nonetheless insisted that government policies protect and promote human dignity. In doing so, they are not "legislating from the bench" or "engaging in judicial lawmaking" or overstepping the bounds of their judicial authority. They are, rather, insisting that a constitutional system be based on fundamental principles of humanity, decency, and the primacy of individual personhood.

In Germany, the Constitutional Court has, in a series of land-mark decisions, obligated the national government to set minimum pensions at a level sufficient to ensure that each person can live with dignity:

> The fundamental right to guarantee a subsistence minimum that is in line with human dignity, . . . ensures every needy person the material conditions that are indispensable for his or her physical existence and for a minimum participation in social, cultural and political life.[26]

In Colombia, the Constitutional Court has insisted that all authorities, including local governments, "guide their actions toward the fulfillment of . . . the promotion of conditions of dignity for all persons, and the resolution of real inequalities that are present in the society, with an eye to establish a just order."[27] The US Supreme Court has refused to recognize poverty as a condition warranting special judicial concern, thus missing the opportunity to hold government to a standard of dignity. To do so would neither violate the Constitution nor lead the courts into the domain of the political branches. The court's job is to ensure that government policies respect human dignity, at all times and under all circumstances. The government's job is to figure out how to do that. This is essentially what the American Bar Association means when it says that "human dignity—the inherent, equal, and inalienable worth of every person—is foundational to a just rule of law" and that "'dignity rights'—the principle that human dignity is fundamental to all areas of law and policy—[should] be reflected in the exercise of [all] legislative, executive, and judicial functions."[28] There is a role for government in designing and enforcing economic policies that protect dignity, and there is a role for courts in ensuring that governments adopt those measures (and don't let them expire). We just need to hold as our lodestar the ability of every person to live with dignity, just as each of us would like to do.

Dignity as Inclusion

The interconnected problems of poverty in America pose a serious threat to the ability of a person to live with dignity. This is true not only for the reasons discussed but also because poverty functions as an excluder. In that sense, poverty is a new Jim Crow. Like the Jim Crow system that characterized American life from the 1870s to the 1960s, poverty now separates people and makes pariahs out of large swaths of our population. The Center for American Progress notes that lack of education makes people less likely to vote, to volunteer, and to donate to charity—all forms of civic and social engagement. Indeed, there is a persistent gap in voter turnout between those in high income brackets and those in low income brackets: according to the Washington Center for Economic Growth, "about 65 percent of low-income individuals voted, compared to 88 percent of those in the high-income category."[29]

This is why the German Constitutional Court insists on a standard of living that is not only adequate for a person's "physical existence" but also for "a minimum participation in social, cultural and political life."[30] This is why the Indian Supreme Court has explained that the minimum necessities for people to live with dignity include the ability to express "oneself in diverse forms, freely moving about and mixing and comingling with fellow human beings," along with adequate nutrition, clothing, and shelter.[31] Dignity is inclusion; it is engagement; it is participation. And we make the choice every day whether or not to ensure that every member of society can live with dignity.

SEVEN

Facing Down the Environmental Apocalypse

The Dignity Impacts of Climate Change

Climate change is real, it's here, it's now, and it's intensifying. It isn't something that's happening to other people, in other places, who lead different kinds of lives. This chapter cannot provide a comprehensive analysis of the impacts of climate change in the United States; its purpose is more modest: simply to show how climate change is harming people and how shifts in political and judicial responses could enhance people's ability to live with dignity.

- "[Some] 14.5 million homes were impacted by natural disasters in 2021, which amounts to one in 10 homes in the United States."[1]

- Nearly two-thirds (62 percent) of US adults say that climate change is noticeably affecting their local communities, and a majority also see climate change as causing serious effects right now.[2]

- "13 percent of Americans reported economic hardship from disasters or severe weather events within the past year."[3]

- "Workers lose about 2% of their weekly paychecks for each day over 90 degrees Fahrenheit, [which amounts] to a roughly $30 pay cut for each day over 90 degrees."

- "Warming is expected to raise global inflation by 0.3 to 1.2 percentage points per year, on average, by 2035 [and] over half the U.S. annual inflation target (about 2% a year) may potentially be attributable just to climate impact."[4]

In August 2024, two towns in the Northeast experienced one thousand year floods—levels of flooding that are statistically expected to happen only once in one thousand years.[5] In September 2024, Hurricane Helene—a "monster storm" bringing "biblical devastation" in what became a "worst-case scenario" to the residents of six states—resulted in hundreds of people losing their lives and thousands struggling to maintain their dignity, with monetary damage costing Americans anywhere from $35 billion (Axios) to $250 billion (PBS).[6] In October, Hurricane Milton slammed down on the coast of Florida (one of the states hit by Helene) in what the Weather Channel called a "devastating," "catastrophic," and "historic" storm, putting up to 5.5 million people under evacuation orders.[7] Both hurricanes were also described as causing one-thousand-year floods. Earlier in 2024, Governor Ron DeSantis once again signed legislation scrubbing the word "climate" from the state's legal regime, despite polls showing that a "majority of Floridians believe in climate change and want action."[8]

In a forty-eight-page report, *The Impact of Climate Change on American Household Finances*, the US Department of the Treasury identified these significant categories of impacts: lost earnings and access to employee benefits, lost or limited access to public benefits programs (on which more than one-third of

Americans rely), property damage and destruction, higher prices for consumer products, increased spending on energy, disruptions to dependent care, increased transportation cost and reduced availability, challenges with health-care access and expenses, challenges accessing funds, insurance gaps, and reduced availability and increased cost of credit.[9] With respect just to lost earnings and access to employee benefits, the Treasury Department report explains:

> Climate events such as flooding and wildfires can damage businesses, as well as key infrastructure such as power systems, roads, and internet service. Moreover, hazards like wildfires or heat waves have the potential to create unsafe working or operational conditions that necessitate closures of businesses and infrastructure. Workers in areas impacted by these hazards may face income loss due to reduced working hours, job loss, or furlough, or could be forced to spend time away from work due to illness or injury. Further, prolonged exposure to climate hazards such as extreme heat can impair workers' physical and cognitive abilities, which can lower their overall productivity and, consequently, result in a decline in their earnings. Over the longer term, recurring climate hazards, like wildfires or heatwaves, could prolong financial strain by reducing available jobs in certain sectors, potentially extending unemployment into months or years. Interruptions in employment have been shown to have persistent, negative impacts on workers' long-term earnings. Adding to these challenges, prolonged time away from work may cause workers to lose access to employer-provided health insurance benefits, income replacement or paid leave, and employee assistance programs.[10]

And these are just the economic impacts that Treasury maps. According to the *Fifth National Climate Assessment*, a congressionally mandated interagency effort that provides the scientific foundation for policy making, "The US now experiences, on average, a billion-dollar weather or climate disaster every three weeks."[11] Every three weeks! The report notes that "climate change is happening now in all regions of the US," mapping how, in each region of the country, each additional increment of warming leads to greater risks in water supply, food security, infrastructure, health and well-being, ecosystems, economy, livelihoods, and heritage.

The report also notes the inequities of climate change impacts:

> For example, areas that were historically redlined—a practice in which lenders avoided providing services to communities, often based on their racial or ethnic makeup—continue to be deprived of equitable access to environmental amenities like urban green spaces that reduce exposure to climate impacts. These neighborhoods can be as much as 12°F hotter during a heatwave than nearby wealthier neighborhoods.
>
> As the climate changes, increased instabilities in US and global food production and distribution systems are projected to make food less available and more expensive. These price increases and disruptions are expected to disproportionately affect the nutrition and health of women, children, older adults, and low-wealth communities.
>
> People who regularly struggle to afford energy bills—such as rural, low-income, and older fixed-income households and communities of color—are especially vulnerable to more intense extreme heat events and associated health risks, particularly if they live in homes with poor insulation and inefficient cooling systems.[12]

And whatever harms men are exposed to are exacerbated for women and girls, who are likely to be more stressed by caregiving, poorer, and more vulnerable to sexual exploitation. The Biden administration has acknowledged this in its "United States Strategy to Respond to the Effects of Climate Change on Women 2023":

> Research shows that climate change does not affect women and men equally, with women suffering disproportionate impacts and experiencing underrepresentation in climate decision-making in all sectors and at all levels, which reduces the likelihood of their perspectives being incorporated and limits outcomes for all of society. Climate change impacts are also compounded for women and girls of color, Indigenous women and girls, women and girls with disabilities, and LGBTQI+ persons, among others.[13]

The climate assessment's focus on health impacts is also instructive:

> Climate change is already harming human health across the US, and impacts are expected to worsen with continued warming. Climate change harms individuals and communities by exposing them to a range of compounding health hazards, including the following: More severe and frequent extreme events; Wider distribution of infectious and vector-borne pathogens; Air quality worsened by smog, wildfire smoke, dust, and increased pollen; Threats to food and water security; and Mental and spiritual health stressors.[14]

But the harms also cut across race, gender, ethnicity, and political lines: "Coastal communities across the country—home to 123 million people (40% of the total US population)—are exposed to sea level rise with millions of people at risk of being displaced from their homes by the end of the century."[15] And according to a 2023 opinion report by Samantha Montano of the *New York Times*,

> The emotional toll of recovery is breaking people. Researchers have found that the circumstances of disaster recovery help to explain increases in domestic violence, a range of mental health issues, worsening physical health in people with pre-existing conditions and suicide. With climate change and its effects accelerating and intensifying, this post-disaster hell is one in which more people in more places are going to find themselves. Our system isn't ready.[16]

The impacts of climate change are striking all parts of the United States in ways that are unpredictable—we never know where the next wildfire will break out or where the path of a hurricane will be, as Helene made abundantly clear. But at the same time, we know exactly where the infrastructure is weakest, where the environment is most vulnerable, and where people have fewer resources to draw on. We know where disasters are most likely to strike and where people will have the biggest challenges in maintaining their dignity when they do.

Miami furnishes a near-apocalyptic example. As *The Atlantic* reports,

> "Rain bombs" are products of our hotter world; warmer air has more room between its molecules for moisture. That water is coming for greater Miami and the 6 million people who live here. This glittering city was built on a drained swamp and sits atop porous limestone; as the sea keeps rising, the National Oceanic and Atmospheric Administration forecasts that South Florida could see almost 11 extra inches of ocean by 2040. Sunny-day flooding, when high tides gurgle up and soak low-lying ground, have increased 400 percent since 1998, with a significant increase after 2006; a major hurricane strike with a significant storm surge could displace up to 1 million people. And with every passing year, the region's infrastructure seems more ill-equipped to deal with these dangers, despite billions of dollars spent on adaptation.[17]

But it's not just Miami. In a report about massive flooding in the Midwest and the upper Plains, the *Washington Post* reports that "around the country, infrastructure is being tested by new precipitation extremes. Even under the most optimistic forecasts, the number of extreme precipitation events is expected to rise dramatically in the upper Plains—and even more so in other parts of the country."[18]

In a four-part report called "The Drowning South," the *Washington Post* shows that the southern United States has one of the fastest-rising coastlines in the world:

> The rapid burst of sea level rise has struck a region spanning from Brownsville, Tex., to Cape Hatteras, N.C., where coastal counties are home to 28 million people. Outdated infrastructure built to manage water, some of it over a century old, cannot keep up. As a result, the seas are swallowing coastal land, damaging property, submerging septic tanks and making key roads increasingly impassable.[19]

As one person who works on local climate resilience initiatives explained, "Each inch up of sea level rise reduces the effectiveness of our storm water to drain and the only place left for it to go is into our roads, yards, homes and businesses."[20] And in the septic tanks. The *Post* devoted one part of this series to the problem of septic tanks, which are widely relied on throughout this region. As the *Post* explains, "To work properly, septic systems need to sit above an adequate amount of dry soil that can filter contaminants from wastewater before it reaches local waterways and underground drinking water sources. But in many communities, that buffer is vanishing."[21] With increased frequency and severity of storms, combined with rising sea levels, the septic system of the southern United States is at risk. The point need not be belabored here, but suffice it to say, it's hard to live with dignity when the septic system fails.

What Policies Will Protect Dignity in the Present Climate Emergency?

In the area of environmental and climate policy, there is a wide gap between what Americans want and what Americans get. This gap could be narrowed if we approach the problems with dignity.

What Americans Want

Let's start with the basics. When climate emergencies strike, they affect people's health and well-being. But American health care is not adequate or equitably available under the best of circumstances, let alone when people are struggling from the effects of climate change. According to KFF,

> About four in ten adults (41%) report having debt due to medical or dental bills including debts owed to credit cards, collections agencies, family and friends, banks, and other lenders to pay for their health care costs, with disproportionate shares of Black and

Hispanic adults, women, parents, those with low incomes, and un-
insured adults saying they have health care debt.

About three in four adults say they are either "very" or "somewhat worried" about being able to afford unexpected medical bills
(74%) or the cost of health care services (73%) for themselves and
their families. Additionally, about half of adults would be unable to
pay an unexpected medical bill of $500 in full without going into
debt.[22]

And this is before the climate emergency strikes. If they
can't get affordable health care, at least they want insurance,
although health insurance—while significantly improved under
the Affordable Care Act—is still not a panacea. KFF reports that
48 percent of insured American adults "worry about affording
their monthly health insurance premium and large shares of
adults with employer-sponsored insurance and those with Marketplace coverage rate their insurance as 'fair' or 'poor' when it
comes to their monthly premium and to out-of-pocket costs to
see a doctor."[23]

Congress could of course fix this, which is what Americans
want. Some "57% say government should ensure health coverage
for all in U.S.,"[24] and about a third of Americans favor a single
payer system (sometimes in the United States referred to as
"Medicare for all"), as most other industrialized nations have,[25]
over the mix of public and private insurers we now have.[26]

Insurance to cover the costs of damage to property is also
often a luxury that most people can't afford and is often limited. After Helene hit the mountains of North Carolina, NBC
reported that "about 2% of residences in the hardest-hit counties
were covered. In North Carolina, that number was 0.7% . . . and
in South Carolina, . . . 0.3%."[27]

Even for those who could afford it, insurance to cover climate emergencies is often not available. As the *Washington Post*
reports,

Americans face another challenge when it comes to severe weather events: getting compensated for their losses. Only about half of the property damage from recent severe weather events in the United States was insured, the study said, and at the same time, large insurers have started halting policies on properties that are in flood- or wildfire-prone areas. Some insurers have stopped offering home insurance policies in California, which has seen numerous large wildfires in the past few years. Others no longer offer coverage for areas that are within a certain distance of the coastline. The insurance policies that remain have become more expensive.[28]

Congress could fix this, too. It could regulate the insurance industry to require the issuance of certain kinds of policies and to reduce or eliminate limitations on climate-related policies. Regulatory policies that would ensure that people could afford the insurance they need to give them peace of mind would help people live with dignity by reducing the emotional toll that climate events invariably exert.

If people cannot avoid the disasters or be insured when they do occur, they at least want the government to help them when there is a disaster, including a climate disaster. By the midpoint of 2024, the Federal Emergency Management Agency (FEMA) had already dispensed more than half a billion dollars in emergency assistance to Americans and issued an average of slightly more than two disaster declarations for states and counties *each week* of 2024.[29] And by most accounts, that barely scratches the surface. As described in the 2023 opinion report by the *New York Times*, "In the past decade, millions of disaster survivors who have applied for individual assistance through FEMA have been denied. According to a Government Accountability Office report, common justifications for denial are a lack of damage to property, lack of evidence of the damage or FEMA's inability to inspect the property. Even when people qualify for relief, they rarely receive enough to make them whole."[30]

Congress has the tools to fix this, too. First, it could fund

FEMA appropriately. "Congress has an opportunity to allow FEMA to give more money to more people more quickly and with fewer restrictions," writes Samantha Montano in her *New York Times* opinion report.[31] But it's not just the money, although the money is clearly critical. Montano continues: "While Congress bears much of the responsibility for recovery reform, FEMA could minimize the administrative burden placed on survivors. Small changes like extending application deadlines—which can range from a couple of weeks to over a year for a major disaster—until after survivors have had time to settle with their insurance companies would help more of them get access to FEMA funding."[32] In other words, Congress could help ensure that the government act with compassion and concern toward the people it is charged with helping. It could provide the funding for both payouts and administration to ensure that survivors have the wherewithal to live with dignity, even in the wake of serious climate disasters. Moreover, as Montano suggests, Congress could "move the agency out of the Department of Homeland Security and restore it to its pre-9/11 status as an independent, cabinet-level entity," which would "minimize the bureaucracy it has to operate within,"[33] thereby connecting more closely with the people it is designed to help and work with. These are simple ways that the government could ensure that people are treated with dignity and live dignified lives. This would help reduce the additional stress-related impacts on the health of climate disaster survivors.

Beyond these specific fixes, there is a very broad consensus in America that the government needs to do more on climate change. According to a 2020 survey from the Pew Research Center, "At a time when partisanship colors most views of policy, broad majorities of the public—including more than half of Republicans and overwhelming shares of Democrats—say they would favor a range of initiatives to reduce the impacts of climate change, including large-scale tree planting efforts, tax credits for businesses that capture carbon emissions and tougher fuel efficiency standards for vehicles."[34] This tracks the Yale Program on Climate Change Communication, which reports that "57% of registered voters would prefer to vote for a candidate for public office who supports action on global warming,"[35] including the vast majority of Democrats and younger Republicans: "Two-thirds of Republicans under age 30 (67%) prioritize the development of alternative energy sources [while] 75% of Republicans ages 65 and older prioritize expanding the production of oil, coal and natural gas."[36] Polls of Floridians, where the law disclaims the existence of climate problems, are consistent: "Floridians overwhelmingly support more government action to address the impacts of climate change, with 69 percent support for state action and 70 percent support for federal action."[37]

So this isn't a situation like some others discussed in this book where Americans are divided on the outcome: everyone wants people to be able to live with dignity in whatever climate conditions exist. So why don't our policies reflect this consensus?

What Americans Get

Legally, America is a complex country. We have a federal government and fifty state governments (plus governance of the District of Columbia, Puerto Rico, and certain outlying territories). The relationship between the federal government and the states is itself complex, in some ways outlined in the Constitution, in some ways left to the experience of more than two hundred years of federal government, and in almost all ways exacerbated by the Supreme Court.

In a very rare victory for environmentalists, the Supreme Court in 2007 "conclusively established that greenhouse gases qualify as air pollutants under the Clean Air Act," thus empowering the Environmental Protection Agency (EPA) to regulate greenhouse gases. This would seem to be a good thing, but over the last ten years, and recently at an accelerating pace, the Court has consistently withheld authority from the EPA and Congress to protect the people and the environment, in favor of private interests.[38] In 2022, the Court held that the EPA did not have the authority to regulate carbon emissions from power plants.[39] In 2023, the Court limited the EPA's authority to protect wetlands, a holding that was said to have the potential for a "catastrophic" effect on the federal government's ability to protect wetlands throughout the country,[40] which increases the risks associated with climate change. As the Natural Resources Defense Council explains, "By regulating water flow, [wetlands] dramatically lessen the impact of both floods and droughts[,] while storing massive amounts of carbon in their abundant vegetation—making safeguarding wetlands a valuable natural climate solution."[41] Then, in 2024, the Court issued a double whammy. On one June day, the Court held that the "E.P.A. could not limit smokestack pollution that blows across state borders," despite evidence that the states at issue "all significantly contributed to ozone pollution in downwind States."[42] The following day, the Court dealt a death blow to the forty-year-old practice of deferring to agency administrators in their interpretation of their statutes. The logic of what was called *Chevron* deference, after the 1984 case in which it was announced, is that unless Congress has restricted agency authority, the agency has the authority and the expertise to make rules; after all, it is the civil service who work at the agencies who know more than anyone else in the government where roads should go, what conditions are necessary to ensure that meat is safe to eat, what warning labels should be on medications and toys, and everything else the government does. The *Chevron* case had been cited more than eighteen thousand times by the federal courts, but the

Supreme Court held that the rule of the case was "unworkable" and that its "continuing import is far from clear."[43] If Congress were more effective, this would not be a big deal; it just needs to be clearer in its legislative authority to the EPA about what it wants the EPA to do. From the standpoint of democracy, this is good, because it puts the onus on the one part of government that is directly democratically accountable—members of Congress. But from a practical standpoint, it's probably disastrous because it subjects the agencies to even more litigation for just doing what they are set up to do and what people want them to do—in this case, protect them from environmental degradation and climate change.

Procedurally as well, the Supreme Court has more often closed the doors to the courthouse than opened them: it has developed extraordinarily high barriers to establish standing, for instance, and has never developed the kinds of procedures accepted in many other countries to hold government accountable, particularly for environmental harms. The most prominent example of this is the ten-year struggle of twenty-one youths who filed a claim against President Barack Obama (restyled against each successive president since then) to get the federal courts to recognize that the rights to life, liberty, and property include the right to a climate capable of sustaining human life. The Ninth Circuit agreed on the urgent need for the government to act. It noted that a "substantial evidentiary record documents that the federal government has long promoted fossil fuel use despite knowing that it can cause catastrophic climate change, and that failure to change existing policy may hasten an environmental apocalypse."[44]

> Copious expert evidence establishes that this unprecedented rise stems from fossil fuel combustion and will wreak havoc on the Earth's climate if unchecked. . . . The hottest years on record all fall within this decade, and each year since 1997 has been hotter than the previous average. . . . The problem is approaching the point of

no return. Absent some action, the destabilizing climate will bury cities, spawn life-threatening natural disasters, and jeopardize critical food and water supplies.[45]

Moreover, the court found, the government's responsibility for the climate emergency is the result of both inaction and action: "The government affirmatively promotes fossil fuel use in a host of ways, including beneficial tax provisions, permits for imports and exports, subsidies for domestic and overseas projects, and leases for fuel extraction on federal land."[46]

It even held that the federal government's decades-long support of fossil fuels had "caused" the actual and real physical, emotional, and mental injuries of which the young plaintiffs complained.[47]

> The plaintiffs' alleged injuries are caused by carbon emissions from fossil fuel production, extraction, and transportation. A significant portion of those emissions occur in this country; the United States accounted for over 25% of worldwide emissions from 1850 to 2012, and [in 2020] accounts for about 15%. And, the plaintiffs' evidence shows that federal subsidies and leases have increased those emissions. About 25% of fossil fuels extracted in the United States come from federal waters and lands, an activity that requires authorization from the federal government.[48]

Yet, backed up by the Supreme Court, the Ninth Circuit court ultimately dismissed the case with finality, without allowing a trial on the merits, finding that addressing climate change is simply beyond the power of the judiciary.[49]

> The plaintiffs have made a compelling case that action is needed; it will be increasingly difficult in light of that record for the political branches to deny that climate change is occurring, that the government has had a role in causing it, and that our elected officials have a moral responsibility to seek solutions. We do not dispute that the broad judicial relief the plaintiffs seek could well goad the political branches into action. We reluctantly conclude, however, that the plaintiffs' case must be made to the political branches or to the electorate at large, the latter of which can change the composi-

tion of the political branches through the ballot box. That the other branches may have abdicated their responsibility to remediate the problem does not confer on Article III courts, no matter how well-intentioned, the ability to step into their shoes.[50]

Let's put aside for the moment the irrational insult to the dignity of young people of denying them the right to vote and then telling them to make their case to the political branches. And let's put aside the insult to their dignity of forcing them to grow into adulthood while they wait just to have their day in court: the wrangling has not been about the right to a stable climate but about whether a federal court can hold a trial on whether there is such a right.

Let's focus instead on some of the other ways in which the US courts are bucking global trends. First, American courts are notoriously insular. They have been resistant to the tide that has swept most other constitutional courts to integrate international, especially international human rights, law into its domestic constitutionalism. This is particularly pronounced in the context of environmental and climate justice where courts from Peru to Pakistan have promoted climate justice. In just 2024, the International Court of Justice, the European Court of Human Rights, the International Tribunal on the Law of the Sea, and the Inter-American Court of Human Rights have issued significant opinions on the obligations of states in the face of climate change, along with several national courts. Even the UK Supreme Court has held that a local city council must "require the environmental impact assessment for a project of crude oil extraction for commercial purposes to include an assessment of the impacts of downstream greenhouse gas emissions resulting from the eventual use of the refined products of the extracted oil."[51]

The US courts' resistance to climate and environmental justice is part of a broader story about US exceptionalism and constitutional interpretation. First, on the side of rights: the US Constitution famously lists very few rights. Unlike almost every constitution on earth, it does not mention human dignity. Nor, unlike about half the world's constitutions, does it include environmental rights or social rights such as rights to health care, education, and shelter. Frankly, it doesn't even outlaw slavery. So the plaintiffs in a climate case have to twist their claims into the narrow openings that the Constitution makes available, notably under the due process clauses or the right to equal protection of the Fifth and Fourteenth Amendments—the intersection of which is where dignity is most likely found.[52]

Second, on the side of congressional power to act: this too is narrow and has been further limited by the Supreme Court, contrary to the increasingly expansive notion of the role of government that exists in the rest of the world. While in the late nineteenth and early twentieth centuries, the Supreme Court sometimes restricted federal power to regulate people's behavior, supporting a laissez-faire state, it largely abandoned that effort in 1937, leaving to the political process the decision about what Congress should and should not regulate. The Court basically said that as long as Congress's decision was rational, it was for the people to decide what they wanted Congress to address. And want they did. For about sixty years, Congress enacted, and the Supreme Court allowed, a spate of laws, including most of the New Deal, social welfare programs including Medicaid and Medicare, environmental regulation including the establishment of the EPA, workplace regulations relating to fair pay and occupational health and safety, civil rights protections for women and minorities, protections for consumers, and much more. But in a 1995 case that invalidated a federal law prohibiting gun possession near schools, the Supreme Court signaled that it was reengaging in the project to limit federal power.[53] Indeed, the

Court has consistently and persistently held that the federal government has no general power to act simply to improve the lives of people or to respond to social challenges.[54] This is a line the Court has energetically policed for the last twenty-five years: judicial activism to prevent the federal government from addressing social issues to protect and enhance people's lives.

But the Court has not fully restricted the power of Congress to act; rather, it has made it more limited and more costly. Instead of allowing Congress to regulate (as it did in the mid-twentieth century), the modern Court has encouraged Congress to accomplish its goals through its power to tax Americans and then spend their money. Using its spending power, Congress can offer financial benefits to those who choose a certain course of conduct over another—essentially offering carrots to those who change their behavior rather than using sticks against those who do not, as direct regulation might do. For instance, in the last few years, Congress has used its spending power to accomplish systemic health-care reform,[55] respond to the economic crisis resulting from COVID,[56] and improve infrastructure.[57] In a certain sense, this advances dignity by limiting regulatory compulsion and enhancing opportunities for agency and reasoned decision-making by individuals. In the climate context, we know that waiting for the national government to respond with legislation or regulations just produced more climate change.

A Market-Based Approach to Climate Change: The Inflation Reduction Act of 2022

In 2022, the US Congress adopted landmark legislation, the Inflation Reduction Act (IRA), designed to mitigate and adapt to the impacts of climate change in a way that does not raise questions about constitutional federal power, adheres to American signature faith in the markets over faith in government regulation to solve social problems, and is aligned with American sensibilities about the size and role of the federal government. It's a huge government program, but it's not regulation. According to the Secretary of the Treasury,

> The Inflation Reduction Act is the single most significant legislation to combat climate change in our nation's history, investing a total of $369 billion to help build a clean energy economy. Nearly three-quarters of that climate change investment—an estimated $270 billion—is delivered through tax incentives, putting Treasury at the forefront of this landmark legislation.[58]

Just within the first year, however, Goldman Sachs was estimating that the "$1.2 trillion in federal incentives may encourage up to $3 trillion in private investment over the next decade, resulting in millions of new, well-paying jobs," according to the World Resources Institute.[59]

If jobs—particularly jobs in the green energy sector—are conduits to dignity, then the IRA is surely a galvanizer of dignity. The IRA acts not through command-and-control regulation but rather by incentives. By empowering people to make decisions for themselves as to what businesses they will build and invest in, it promotes dignity as a mean and as an end. With this approach, it is the private sector rather than government that is expected to do the work of reducing carbon emissions.[60] As one analysis explains, "The legislation includes $369 billion for climate and energy provisions and will contribute to reducing carbon emissions from 2005 levels by approximately 40 percent by 2030 by accelerating the decarbonization of electricity production and other carbon-intensive sectors."[61] According to another analysis, it may even enable the United States to meet its nationally determined contributions under the 2015 Paris Agreement.[62] Moreover, the "significant commitment to a sustainable future aligns the legislation with the principles of" Environmental and Social Governance.[63] This will protect human dignity in myriad ways, allowing millions of people to live with their dignity intact, protected from the ravages of climate change.

It will not be known for some time to what extent the economic and environmental promises of the IRA will be fulfilled.[64] As of mid-2024, we do know that the benefits of the act are broadly felt: the Treasury Department has reported that "more than 3.4 million American families have already claimed more than $8 billion in residential clean energy and home energy efficiency credits against their 2023 federal income taxes."[65] And we know that, over the long term, "the IRA will likely still reduce the federal deficit over the decade by about $175 billion and will certainly reduce the deficit even more over the long run."[66]

Still, the future of the law is precarious: while the goals of the IRA are broadly shared among the electorate, and its benefits are distributed throughout the country, interest in and support for the IRA is partisan. Although most Americans want Congress to do more to protect the environment, and the sustainability of the planet and all of its living inhabitants, the electorate is divided and somewhat apathetic when it comes to support for this monumental effort. In polls conducted before the 2024 election, forty-one percent of Americans had heard "nothing at all" about it. Liberal Democrats and conservative Republicans were more likely to have heard "a lot" or "some" about it, while moderate Republicans were least likely to have heard about it.[67]

In 2023, the Yale Program on Climate Change Communication explored this further, giving respondents a brief description of the law. After reading it, 71 percent said they supported it strongly or somewhat. More than nine in ten Democrats supported it, and more than seven in ten liberal or moderate Republicans supported it. That's a lot of bipartisan support! The only group that did not support it after reading the description was conservative Republicans, of whom only 33 percent supported it, "while 66%

oppose it (including 43% who strongly oppose it)." This tracks
with Americans' desires before the IRA was adopted to see Congress act to protect against climate change. It shows broad and
deep support for government action on climate but also divided
opinions among conservatives. This is true even though conservatives are just as likely as liberals to experience climate volatil-
ity and climate disasters, to need government assistance when
they do, and to benefit from congressional and agency efforts to
address climate change.

A Government That Protects Our Dignity

Americans deserve a government that protects them and ensures that they can live with dignity, even as the climate changes.
For a variety of reasons—ranging from manipulation of the political process through gerrymandering, to political procedural
maneuvers, to public disinformation, to the difficulties of life for
most Americans and the complexity of the political process—
American democracy has entered a phase of minority rule,
where the government is failing to represent the interests of the
people. People understand that we have reached the point of environmental apocalypse and institutional collapse where doing
nothing is not an option.

The effects of climate change wreck people's bodies, stress
their spirits, empty their bank accounts, and break their hearts.
It does not violate a singular right contained in a silo of enumerated rights. It affects their ability to live with dignity by impair-
ing an array of rights. We the people deserve better. We deserve
a politics of dignity.

EIGHT

Dignity and Democracy

Voting as an Act of Dignity

Part of human dignity is having agency over one's life and being able to make decisions for how one's life will turn out. In Latin America, this is referred to as having control over one's "life project." People who are living with dignity are able to make decisions for themselves about what they will study, what kind of work they will do, whom they will marry, whether and when and how often (if at all) to have children, and so on. That is why reproductive rights are so important, and so is financial independence. No one can force you inside a box or define you according to their categories. If someone is making these decisions for you, they are treating you with something less than equal dignity.

If you have equal human dignity, you not only get to *be* yourself, but you also get to act and express yourself. You get to openly express your loves (by being "out" with your partner of choice), your passions (by being the artist, the cook, the car mechanic you want to be), your values (by wearing religious symbols or speaking at a city council meeting or joining a protest march).

You get to choose how to identify yourself culturally, ethnically, religiously, sexually, or in any other way, or not.

This is important because people live in community with others. That's obvious, but it's such an important aspect of human dignity, it's worth drawing attention to it—especially in the United States where we glorify individualism and enjoy the myth of the self-made man. Indeed, the idea of dignity is often understood in such individualistic terms: it's inherent in each of us, it's each person's right to define who they are for themselves and by themselves. It's often connected to the idea of autonomy—making rules for oneself. But in reality, no person lives only by their own rules; no one is really self-made. No individual does everything on their own (except for those few hermits who live in cabins in the woods and don't talk to anyone). But most of us live with, depend on, talk to, share with, work with, and love with others. We live in multiple overlapping communities, with our friends, our colleagues, our neighbors, our families, and so on. The rules we live by are rules that our communities make together. So everyone has a dignity right to participate in decision-making for their own community. This is what dignity scholars and jurists call "participatory dignity" or "civic dignity." It's what the rest of us call "we the people."

In our system, voting is the quintessential act of democratic participation. This is why voting is an act of dignity. It is a way to choose the course of our communal life project—to choose for ourselves what values we want, what rules we want to follow, what kind of society we want to live in. So it's critical for our communities—including our national community—and it's critical for each one of us to be able to express our own opinions about our community. Because if we don't decide for ourselves what rules we want to live by, someone else will decide for us. This is the essential difference between a democracy and any other form of government. In a democracy, each adult can decide important questions for themselves as a matter of their inherent human dignity and their "reason and conscience," as the UDHR says. Otherwise, someone else takes that job and makes decisions for the people.

Some people argue that a "benign dictator"—that is, a dictator who makes wonderful decisions for the people—would be all right. But it would still be a violation of human dignity because it would be one person (the hypothetical, never-really-exists-in-real-life nice dictator) making important decisions *for* other people. They would be giving to someone else their dignity right to make decisions for themselves. So even if such a thing existed, it would be better, to protect human dignity, for people to make decisions for themselves, even if those decisions are lousy. Not only does this deposit the power to decide in each one of us, but it gives us the power to change our minds and choose a different course. This isn't something that dictators, benign or not, often do. The power to decide should always rest with the people who are affected.

The United States has always been committed to democracy, but the form of democracy we have is thin and halting. Sure, we have regular elections, and, sure, there are some court cases that talk about the importance of voting and some that even try to make voting more fair and more effective. But for the most part, neither the text of the Constitution nor the Supreme Court has prioritized voting in the United States either as an individual right or as a social necessity. And, in fact, there are increasingly worrisome departures from that dignity-based value.

A thorough explanation of democracy in America is beyond the scope of this book, so the first part of this chapter will only briefly identify some of the ways in which our constitutional law fails to protect the dignity of voting. We then contrast this with language from outside the United States that shows why democracy must be protected as a matter of human dignity. The last section builds on these cases and offers some concrete suggestions for how we could protect the dignity of voting in the United States.

The Undemocratic Constitution

The Constitution does make two democratic advances, radical for the eighteenth century: the people will vote for their elected representatives in the national congress, and they will vote for their head of state. This means that the people who hold sovereign power for us have to earn the honor by gaining the trust of the people. No more monarchies. No dictators. No hereditary office holders: John Quincy Adams and George W. Bush did not become president because their fathers had held the position; they had to win it on their own.

Of course, the framers of the Constitution had some skepticism about democracy as well: the Senate was, until 1912, a body of men who had been appointed by their state legislatures, more or less ensuring that the elites of each state would select their elite brethren to represent their elite interests in Washington. And the Electoral College—an institution unique in modern governance—was devised to ensure that elites, and not the people, would have the ultimate say in who lived in the White House. Out of fifty-nine presidential elections, five have gone to men who did not win the popular vote.[1] Perhaps this explains some of the current disconnect between what the people want and what they get—not only in the context of climate change but in the area of health care and reproductive rights as well.

Moreover, the framers of the federal Constitution did not guarantee any person the right to vote for president. They actually left that to the states. The framers—known for all time for establishing the first and longest-running functioning democracy—apparently didn't trust the people, so they didn't give them a right to vote and didn't trust the federal government they were creating, so they gave the power to regulate elections to the states. There may have been good historical reasons for this in the waning days of the eighteenth century, but it is beyond strange today that the people of the United States don't have a constitutional right to vote for the president of the United States. And it's harder still to explain how the Supreme Court would not have fixed that in the 240 years it has spent interpreting, applying, and adapting the Constitution. But it hasn't.

What federal law has done instead is to prohibit states from discriminating against certain groups of people in the elections it chooses to manage. The post–Civil War Fifteenth Amendment prohibits states from denying any person the right to vote on the basis of race. They can deny any person the right to vote for other reasons, but not on the basis of race. Of course, this permitted the continued disenfranchisement of women for another fifty years, when in 1920, the Constitution finally prohibited discrimination on the basis of gender. Other expansions of the right to vote followed suit, in the same format—not by giving people the right to vote, or ensuring that they could exercise their dignity-based right to vote, but by disallowing states from discriminating on the basis of poverty (Twenty-Fourth Amendment, 1964, eliminating the poll tax that was widely used to disenfranchise African Americans) and age (Twenty-Sixth Amendment, 1971, when the voting age for all elections was lowered to eighteen).[2]

In 1965, Congress passed the Voting Rights Act, perhaps the most progressive piece of legislation ever adopted in America to expand and strengthen democracy, protect the rights of those who were most vulnerable to disenfranchisement, and recognize the inherent dignity of every person to cast a ballot. According to the Supreme Court when it upheld the law in 1966,

The Voting Rights Act was designed by Congress to banish the blight of racial discrimination in voting, which has infected the electoral process in parts of our country for nearly a century. The Act creates stringent new remedies for voting discrimination where it persists on a pervasive scale, and, in addition, the statute strengthens existing remedies for pockets of voting discrimination elsewhere in the country.[3]

One sign of America's lukewarm commitment to voting rights, however, is that this law is unusual in having a sunset clause, unlike most laws that presumptively last. That is actually the purpose of inscribing something into law. But this one requires an affirmative vote of Congress to continue to protect voting rights, and it expires unless Congress repeatedly readopts it. Given that states continued to engage in "serious and widespread" practices of racial discrimination to depress the ability of nonwhites to vote in America, Congress repeatedly reauthorized the law, including in 2006, when it passed the House (390–33) and then the Senate (98–0). Congress had found that the Voting Rights Act had "directly caused significant progress in eliminating first-generation barriers to ballot access, leading to a marked increase in minority voter registration and turnout and the number of minority elected officials." Nonetheless, "second generation barriers constructed to prevent minority voters from fully participating in the electoral process" continued to exist, as well as "racially polarized voting in the covered jurisdictions, which increased the political vulnerability of racial and language minorities in those jurisdictions." Congress concluded that "without the continuation of the Voting Rights Act of 1965 protections, racial and language minority citizens will be deprived of the opportunity to exercise their right to vote, or will have their votes diluted, undermining the significant gains made by minorities in the last 40 years."[4] When President George W. Bush signed the reauthorization a week later; he called it "an example of our continued commitment to a united America where every person is valued and treated with dignity and respect."[5]

This evidence was all before the Supreme Court in 2013 when it reviewed the law in *Shelby County v. Holder*. There, it held, 5–4, that the central provisions of the Voting Rights Act were unnecessary and therefore unconstitutional. Think about that. The "rule of five" is that you only need five votes for the Court to make or break a law, and the people casting their votes are absolutely unaccountable with regard to their vote. In this case, five men (John Roberts, Antonin Scalia, Anthony Kennedy, Clarence Thomas, and Samuel Alito) decided that the president of the United States, 98 senators, and 390 members of the House of Representatives were wrong to give federal protection to people who wanted to vote in federal elections. It's astounding.

The desired results were immediate. The crux of the Voting Rights Act was that states with histories of racial vote suppression had to seek "pre-clearance" from the federal Department of Justice before an electoral law could go into effect to ensure that the new law did not dilute minority voting rights. *Shelby* essentially eliminated that federal oversight, allowing states to adopt whatever laws their legislatures saw fit, including laws that would disempower and disenfranchise minorities and others. As the Voting Rights Lab explains it, "For 50 years, the VRA protected voter access by blocking strict photo ID laws with a discriminatory impact from going into effect. With the *Shelby* decision, a deluge of those laws took effect in the states that were previously covered." Some laws were enacted right after *Shelby*, and "some were intentionally enacted in anticipation of the decision, taking effect after the fact"—sometimes within hours of the decision.[6]

The *Shelby* decision also allowed restrictions on mail-in voting to go into effect. Mail-in voting is especially useful for people who are restricted in their mobility and people who have limited time or resources. Of the fifteen states subject to the preclearance requirement under the Voting Rights Act, twelve have passed laws restricting the ability of people to vote by mail (including five after the 2020 elections).[7] Five states have "passed legislation searching for non-citizens for voter list removal without any examination to ensure these new laws do not have a discriminatory impact on citizens of color."[8] These laws are both racially motivated and politically partisan since, historically, voters who are citizens of color tend to prefer Democrat candidates over Republican ones.

The American system is committed in principle to letting the people decide who will speak for them in government, but it does not fully trust the people, both for historical reasons (the elite framers didn't much trust the nonelite, the nonwhite, the nonmale, the nonpropertied) and for ongoing reasons manifested in our policies about who gets to vote and how those votes are counted. This lack of trust in "the people" is just another way of saying that the dignity of all is not equally respected. Many other countries—both countries where democracy is well established and countries that are struggling to embed democratic ways—recognize the tight connection between dignity and democracy.

Dignity and Democracy Abroad

The rest of the world has learned a lot from American-style democracy. About half the constitutions of the world, from Afghanistan and Angola to Zambia and Zimbabwe, begin with the phrase "We the people . . ." Everyone gets that government legitimacy rests on the consent of the governed, and if anyone is going to give sovereign power to a state or a government, it is going to be "the people" of that state. That is the essence of democracy—government by the people, for the people, and of the people. That's not only good for government; it's good for people too because it's how people express that part of their dignity that seeks to control the course of their lives and shape their social environment.

The constitutional courts of a number of countries have made the link between dignity and democracy explicit. Here are just three examples, from countries with vastly different cultural and political traditions.

Perhaps the most prominent example of the recognition of democratic dignity is from South Africa. Shortly after the end of apartheid, a couple of prisoners argued to the Constitutional Court that the elections commission's failure to enable them to vote while in prison violated the Constitution. The Court agreed. South Africa's 1996 Constitution guarantees that "every adult citizen has the right to vote in elections for any legislative body established in terms of the Constitution, and to do so in secret."[9] The Court explained why, in the new South Africa, this provision and others reinforcing the commitment to democracy were so important.

> Universal adult suffrage on a common voters roll is one of the foundational values of our entire constitutional order. The achievement of the franchise has historically been important both for the acquisition of the rights of full and effective citizenship by all South Africans regardless of race, and for the accomplishment of an all-embracing nationhood. The universality of the franchise is important not only for nationhood and democracy. The vote of each and every citizen is a badge of dignity and of personhood. Quite literally, it says that everybody counts.[10]

Voting is a badge of dignity and personhood. If everybody votes, everybody counts. As the same Court said in another case, "Participation is necessary to preserve human dignity and self respect."[11] It refers to this as "civic dignity."

The Court in the prison voting case explained that voting is critical not only to legitimize the government, and not only to respect individual dignity, but also for social cohesion: "In a country of great disparities of wealth and power it declares that whoever we are, whether rich or poor, exalted or disgraced, we all belong to the same democratic South African nation; that our destinies are intertwined in a single interactive polity."[12] Certainly the same could be true of America today: with its deep cultural, political, and economic divisions, voting is more important now than ever.

The South African Court concluded with an important mandate: "Rights may not be limited without justification and legislation dealing with the franchise must be interpreted in favour of enfranchisement rather than disenfranchisement."[13] This is a command to the government and to all other courts to presume, protect, and promote the ability of people to vote as a matter of national unity and individual dignity.

Next we turn to Pakistan, a place that you might not think of as the paragon of democracy. But some of its judges have been at the vanguard of protecting individual rights, precisely because it is of such critical importance in places that struggle with democracy and governmental legitimacy. Justice Syed Mansoor Ali Shah, who now sits on that country's Supreme Court, is globally recognized for his judicial commitment to dignity-based law. While he was on the High Court of Lahore, he explained how liberty, dignity, and democracy are all intertwined. In a case involving gerrymandering, he wrote that the life of a citizen in a representative democracy

> cannot be envisaged without its political dimension; the ability to participate in the political life of the nation, the freedom to exercise political choice, the right to choose a political leader and elect the

government of his or her choice. Liberty means not only freedom
from government coercion but also the freedom to participate in
the government itself.[14]

In the modern world, liberty includes the freedom to participate in the government itself. One hundred years ago, Justice
Brandeis wrote that those who won our independence "valued
liberty both as an end, and as a means."[15] Since then, the Supreme Court has struggled mightily to discern what liberty actually includes, but it has failed to say that it includes the right to
vote. The Pakistan Supreme Court explains why it must:

> In a constitutional democracy, a vote is a symbol of political dignity
> and freedom of a citizen. It embodies freedom of choice, expres-
> sion, equality and the license to participate in the political life of
> a nation and the right to establish self-government. [The life] of a
> citizen in a representative democracy demands a life of equal par-
> ticipation in the establishment of a democratic state.[16]

What's interesting is that, as in South Africa, this form
of "political dignity" operates both at the level of individual
rights—the right of each person to choose, to express ideas, and
to participate—and at the level of the structure of the state. It's
both an individual dignity right and a necessity if the state is
going to have a legitimate government.

Our third example comes from Germany, where the Constitutional Court has also insisted on the relationship between dignity and democracy. In a case involving the constitutionality of
the proposed European Constitution, the Court explained that
"the citizens' right to determine in respect of persons and subjects, in freedom and equality by means of elections and other
votes, public authority is the fundamental element of the principle of democracy. The right to free and equal participation in
public authority is enshrined in human dignity."[17]

More recently, the German Court considered whether an

anti-Semitic, neo-Nazi party could be banned from the political process. The Court found that the party's platform of "anti-semitic concepts or other concepts aimed at race discrimination are incompatible with human dignity and thus violate the free democratic order."[18] It explained the stark connection between the democratic order and human dignity:

> The free democratic order is rooted primarily in human dignity. Human dignity is not subject to disposition and the state must respect and protect it in all forms. In particular the safeguard of human dignity protects personal individuality, identity and integrity, and elementary equality before the law.[19]

Here, the Court is emphasizing the importance of the government respecting human dignity by ensuring that its political system treats every person as a person. "Human dignity is egalitarian, it is founded exclusively in the fact that a person belongs to the human race, regardless of origin, race, age or gender."[20] In the end, the Court said that the neo-Nazi party could not be banned "because it is unlikely they will succeed in their political aim," given their failures at the polls up to that point, in 2017.[21]

We see this perspective only sporadically in the case law of the US Supreme Court. In a political free speech case, the Court said that the Constitution puts

> the decision as to what views shall be voiced largely into the hands of each of us, in the hope that use of such freedom will ultimately produce a more capable citizenry and more perfect polity and in the belief that no other approach would comport with the premise of individual dignity and choice upon which our political system rests.[22]

But as we have seen, American democracy is not fully realized.

How We Could Protect the Dignity of Voting

This is not complicated. We ensure that every person has the right to vote, that all voters are able to exercise that right on a free and equal basis, and that every vote is counted.

Ensuring that every person has the right to vote may involve both positive and negative actions on the part of the government. In the United States, we seem to have a cultural or political preference for negative rights over positive ones; that is, we say we prefer when government stays out of the way, doesn't get involved, and lets us be free. But often that is not the case: people want reproductive rights protected, they want healthcare options, they want emergency funds when disaster strikes, and they want a better climate policy to prevent so many disasters from striking. They want government to be there when they need it. As voting rights and all these examples make clear, the line between negative rights and positive rights is illusory. People want the government to protect them.

So with respect to voting, we have to both eliminate barriers and facilitate access. Facilitating access is simple and is done in most countries that respect the democratic vote of their citizens. We should hold elections on weekends or public holidays so that working people don't have to take time off from work. More than a third of countries hold elections on Saturdays or (most often) Sundays; many countries that hold elections on weekdays declare those days to be a national holiday.[23] We should ensure that people have access to polling places and ensure that they are open and well staffed; unavailable and inaccessible polling places disproportionately affect poor communities and communities of color.[24] We should expand opportunities to vote by expanding the time frame. This would not only give people more flexibility as to when they vote but would allow vote counters more time to do their work. We should use technology to make our elections more reliable and efficient. And we should expand opportunities for voting other than in person, which is especially helpful for people with fewer resources; if we can bank and pay our taxes online, why can't we vote online? At the same time, we need to eliminate restrictions on who can vote. According to the League of Women Voters, "As of the 2020 election, nearly 29 million voting-age US citizens did not have a valid driver's license, and 7.6 million did not have any other valid form of government ID."[25] Registration should be automatic upon turning eighteen. And we need to eliminate disenfranchisement of people who have committed crimes (which prohibits about 4.6 million people from voting[26]).

These are easy fixes, but they would significantly contribute to the protection of democracy by eliminating barriers on voting. And there are many, many other ways we could, if we wanted, expand opportunities to vote and to otherwise engage in peaceful political activity and strengthen the legitimacy of democratic elections. In this way, our laws would meaningfully protect the dignity of all adults in society.

Expanding Democracy by Protecting Dignity Rights

The crux of it is this: the more we protect human dignity, the more people can engage in the political process, and the broader and stronger our democracy is, and the more we can protect human dignity. Voting and political engagement are, indeed, the source and the purpose of our democratic form of government, the means and the ends.

If the government itself does not protect the dignity right to vote, the courts have an important role to play, as a backstop, to ensure that the democratic process works as openly and legitimately as it can. They can protect the democratic system because it's important to the country and because it's important to the individual human beings in the country. We sometimes balk when courts seem to overstep their bounds. Some people complain when a court appears to protect rights that are not written explicitly in the Constitution. But when courts protect *dignity* rights, they are not going beyond the bounds of the Constitution, they are not aggrandizing their own power, and they are not recalibrating the balance of power. No, it's just the opposite. What they are doing is strengthening democracy. They are building up the public sphere—the sphere where people act as autonomous human beings with agency and free will to design the kinds of communities they want to live in, to control their own lives, to shape their future.

Epilogue

Dignity matters because it matters to people. People know dignity and they understand it. They know their own dignity, their own worth. They think their lives, their opinions, and their values are important. They know that when their dignity is dented or damaged or threatened, an injustice is afoot. And we know it about others too—even if we are not injured in the same way, we know it when we see someone sleeping outside or waiting all day in line to vote, or having to drive to the next state just to get urgent medical care, or is standing waist deep in floodwaters in their living room. We know these are injustices precisely because they are harms to people's dignity; it's just not the way people should live. Dignity evokes the worth in each of us and empathy for each other. And we know that dignity matters, no matter what. That a human being is still a human being, even if they're poor, even if they've committed a crime, even if they've betrayed a friendship; they're still human and should never be treated as anything less than human. When we lose that sense of their humanity, we lose something of our own.

Without dignity, policy decisions are made out of the competition of the available choices: we can ensure equal opportunities to thrive, or not; women can have reproductive rights, or not. We can have a democracy where tens of millions of people are unable to vote, or we can have a democracy where everyone votes. There is no right or wrong, just what a majority of those in power (in any of our three branches of government) want to do for whatever reasons they want to it. It's a horse race, as if we had no horse in the race.

But we do. We are all born equal in dignity and rights. Something happens in the moments, years, decades after birth that enhances the power of some to live with dignity at the expense of others. To return to the state of equal human dignity for all, we need to make sure that our policy choices enhance and protect human dignity and expand the spaces in which human beings can flourish. This is precisely why the American Bar Association says that recognition of dignity is foundational to a "just rule of law."[1]

The promotion of dignity should be the backbone, the guiding principle, the "lodestar" of our democratic system and our society.[2] We should promote human dignity because it's important to everyone. And if we don't protect it, who will?

Gratitudes

I extend thanks to many students at Widener University Delaware Law School who have helped inform, expand, and enrich my understanding of the role of dignity in our legal and political system. Sarah Plasse and Maria Touimi-Benjelloun have provided exceptional research assistance. I am exceedingly grateful to the Law School for supporting my dignity rights work throughout the years.

I would also like to acknowledge Marcela Cristina Maxfield at Stanford University Press, who supported this work and provided wonderful guidance and feedback throughout the process.

Finally, I am deeply indebted to David Williamson, who sparked the idea for this book, and to Les Daly and Eudice Daly, and Jasper Daly-Williamson and Alex Daly-Williamson, who have contributed in more ways than I can say.

Notes

Preface

1. Cohen v. California, 403 U.S. 15, 24 (1971).

2. Obergefell v. Hodges, 576 U.S. 644, 681 (2015).

3. Trop v. Dulles, 356 U.S. 86, 100 (1958).

4. "The New Atlantic Charter," White House, June 10, 2021, https://www.whitehouse.gov/briefing-room/statements-releases/2021/06/10/the-new-atlantic-charter/.

5. Erin Daly, *Dignity Rights: Courts, Constitutions, and the Worth of the Human Person* (Philadelphia: University of Pennsylvania Press, 2012), 104.

Chapter 1

1. Hitlin and Andersson, *The Science of Dignity: Measuring Personhood and Well-Being in the United States* (Oxford: Oxford University Press, 2003), 2.

2. Hitlin and Andersson, *The Science of Dignity*, 2–3.

3. Matthew McManus, *Making Human Dignity Central to International Human Rights Law* (Cardiff: University of Wales Press).

4. Laurie W. Ackermann, *Human Dignity: Lodestar for Equality in South Africa* (Cape Town: Juta, 2012), quoting MEC for Education: KwaZulu-Natal & Others v. Pillay 2008 1 SA 474 (CC), para. 53. See also Erin Daly and James R. May, *Dignity Law: Recognition, Cases, and Perspectives*, quoted in *Casebook* (Buffalo, NY: Hein, 2020), 53.

5. Francis Coralie Mullin v. The Administrator, Union Territory of Delhi, AIR 1981 SC 746.

6. Mubarik Ali Babar v. Punjab Public Service Commission through its Secretary & others, Civil Petition No. 2045 of 2019 at 2–3.

7. United Nations, Charter of the United Nations, Preamble.

8. Glenn Hughes, "The Concept of Dignity in the Universal Declaration of Human Rights," *Journal of Religious Ethics* 39, no. 1 (March 2011): 1–24, at 5; see also Tamara Peicu, "Human Dignity and Human Rights," *Jurnalul Libertății de Conștiință* 2 (2019): 526–537, at 529.

9. Hughes, "Concept of Dignity," 5; see also Peicu, "Human Dignity and Human Rights," 529.

10. "How to Say Dignity in Different Languages," *Indifferent Languages*, 2013–24, https://www.indifferentlanguages.com/words/dignity.

11. Jeremy Waldron, Meir Dan-Cohen, Wai-Chee Dimock, Don Herzog, and Michael Rosen, *Dignity, Rank, and Rights* (New York: Oxford University Press, 2012).

12. "History of the Declaration," United Nations, 2024, https://www .un.org/en/about-us/udhr/history-of-the-declaration.

13. Both covenants were opened for signature in 1966 and went into force in 1976. The United States signed and ratified the International Covenant on Civil and Political Rights in 1992. It has signed the International Covenant on Economic, Social, and Cultural Rights (under President Jimmy Carter), but it remains one of six nations that has not ratified it. International Covenant on Civil and Political Rights, opened for signature December 19, 1966, 999 UNTS 171, entered into force March 23, 1976. United States, signed December 16, 1966, ratified June 8, 1992; and International Covenant on Economic, Social, and Cultural Rights, opened for signature December 19, 1966, 993 UNTS 3, entered into force January 3, 1976. United States, signed October 5, 1977.

14. "The Dignity Rights Case Library," Google Docs, accessed July 17, 2024, https://docs.google.com/spreadsheets/d/1GebYSEqcECDla3V t9Ohw5ivi1Tq9ywFgGwIfdHojg_w/edit#gid=51272552.

15. X v. The Principal Secretary, Health and Family Welfare Department, Govt. of NCT of Delhi & Anr. India Supreme Court, 2022 at paras. 109, 111.

16. AK v. Minister of Police (CCT 94/20) [2022] ZACC 14; 2022 (11) BCLR 1307 (CC); 2023 (1) SACR 113 (CC); 2023 (2) SA 321 (CC) (April 5, 2022).

17. Case of R.R. and R.D. v. Slovakia (Application no. 20649/18) ECtHR, 2020 at para. 146, citing Bouyid v. Belgium [GC], no. 23380/09,

§§ 100–101, September 28, 2015; and "HUDOC—European Court of Human Rights," accessed September 28, 2024, https://hudoc.echr.coe .int/fre?i=001-204154.

18. "HUDOC—European Court of Human Rights," para. 200.

19. Mubarik Ali Babar v. Punjab Public Service Commission, Civil Petition No. 2045 of 2019, Supreme Court of Pakistan, Appellate Jurisdiction, Bench-V, November 18, 2022.

20. R. v. Bissonnette, 2022 SCC 23, para. 59, quoting Quebec (Attorney General) v. 9147-0732 Québec inc., 2020 SCC 32, para. 51 (noting that the Court was unanimous on this point), and citing Ward v. Quebec (Commission des droits de la personne et des droits de la jeunesse), 2021 SCC 43, para. 56; Quebec (Public Curator) v. Syndicat national des employés de l'hôpital St-Ferdinand, [1996] 3 S.C.R. 211, para. 105; and C. Brunelle, "La dignité dans la Charte des droits et libertés de la personne: De l'ubiquité à l'ambiguïté d'une notion fondamentale," *Revue du Barreau* (numéro thématique) 143 (2006): 150–151.

21. "State and Another v Banda and Others [2023] 1 LRC 369.Pdf," Google Docs, accessed July 17, 2024, https://drive.google.com/file/d/ 1UDeCesTo_pEzCq5NGIn2VYolkxl-VR6f/view.

22. Hopkins et al. v. Hosemann, No. 19–60678 (5th Cir. 2023) at 25.

23. Davis v. Neal, 1:21-cv-01773-TLA, 15 (D. Del. Aug. 17, 2023) at 15–17.

24. A.B.A. Resolution 113B (Aug. 2019), *supra* note 4.

25. "Center for Democratic and Environmental Rights," April 30, 2024, https://www.centerforenvironmentalrights.org.

26. United States v. Windsor, 570 U.S. 744, 133 S. Ct. 2675 (2013).

27. Obergefell v. Hodges, 576 U.S. 644, 663 (2015).

28. Obergefell v. Hodges, 576 U.S. 644, 704 (2015) (Roberts J., dissenting).

29. "The primary purpose of the Civil Rights Act of 1964, . . . is the vindication of human dignity and not mere economics." Heart of Atlanta Motel, Inc. v. United States, 379 U.S. 241, 85 S. Ct. 348, 13 L. Ed. 2d 258 (1964) (Goldberg J., concurring).

30. Obergefell v. Hodges, 576 U.S. 644, 735 (2015) (Thomas J., dissenting).

31. X v. The Principal Secretary at para. 116.

32. United Nations, "SDG Indicators," https://unstats.un.org/sdgs/ report/2022/Goal-01/.

Chapter 2

1. United States v. Windsor, 570 U.S. 744, 133 S. Ct. 2675 (2013); and Students for Fair Admissions v. University of North Carolina, citation pending.

2. *SFFA* (Gorsuch, J., dissenting at 3).

3. Plessy v. Ferguson, 163 U.S. 537, 559 (1896) (Harlan J., dissenting).

4. This is such a hard rule that the analogy is not even apt: people who are color-blind still see color; the Court's emphasis here is exclusively on being blind.

5. "About: Students for Fair Admissions," accessed September 28, 2024, https://studentsforfairadmissions.org/about/.

6. "About: Students for Fair Admissions," 35–36.

7. "About: Students for Fair Admissions," 44–45.

8. Brown v. Board of Education of Topeka, 347 U.S. 483, 493 (1954).

9. San Antonio Independent School District v. Rodriguez, 411 U.S. 1 (1973). Some state constitutions provide rights to education.

10. Meyer v. Nebraska, 262 U.S. 390 (1923); and Pierce v. Society of Sisters, 268 U.S. 510 (1925).

11. Wisconsin v. Yoder, 406 U.S. 205 (1972).

12. Iris Hinh, "State Policymakers Should Reject K-12 School Voucher Plans: Proposals Would Undermine Public Schools," Center on Budget and Policy Priorities, March 21, 2023, https://www.cbpp.org/research/state-budget-and-tax/state-policymakers-should-reject-k-12-school-voucher-plans; and Nina Mast, "State and Local Experience Proves School Vouchers Are a Failed Policy That Must Be Opposed," Economic Policy Institute, April 20, 2023, https://www.epi.org/blog/state-and-local-experience-proves-school-vouchers-are-a-failed-policy-that-must-be-opposed-as-voucher-expansion-bills-gain-momentum-look-to-public-school-advocates-for-guidance.

13. "What You Need to Know about the Right to Education," UNESCO, November 26, 2020, https://www.unesco.org/en/articles/what-you-need-know-about-right-education.

14. The preamble to the UDHR also states that the General Assembly "proclaims this Universal Declaration of Human Rights as a common standard of achievement for all peoples and all nations, to the end that every individual and every organ of society, keeping this Declaration constantly in mind, shall strive by teaching and education to promote respect for these rights and freedoms." Accessed October 4, 2024, https://www.un.org/en/about-us/universal-declaration-of-human-rights.

15. Mohini Jain vs. State of Karnataka, 1992, 3 SCC 666 (India).

16. S.T.F. ADPF 186, Relator: Ricardo Lewandowski, 26.04.2012. See also ADPF (Braz.), voto da Senhor Ministro Cezar Peluso, April 26, 2012, https://redir.stf.jus.br/paginadorpub/paginador.jsp?docTP=TP&docID= 6984693.

17. Emily Parker, "50-State Review," March 2016, https://www.ecs.org/wp-content/uploads/2016-Constitutional-obligations-for-public-education-1.pdf.

18. According to the OECD Better Life Index, the United States ranks 19 out of forty-one countries in student skills and 28 out of thirty-nine in social inequality. "OECD Better Life Index," OECD, 2021, https://www.oecdbetterlifeindex.org/topics/education/.

19. Brian D. Smedley, Audrey T. Stith, Leininger Colburn, and Clyde H. Evans, *The Right Thing to Do, the Smart Thing to Do: Enhancing Diversity in the Health Professions: Summary of the Symposium on Diversity in Health Professions in Honor of Herbert W. Nickens, M.D.* (Washington, DC: National Academies Press, 2001); Linda Darling-Hammond, "Inequality in Teaching and Schooling: How Opportunity Is Rationed to Students of Color in America," in Smedley et al., *The Right Thing to Do,* https://www.ncbi.nlm.nih.gov/books/NBK223640/.

20. Smedley et al., *The Right Thing to Do*; Darling-Hammond, "Inequality in Teaching and Schooling."

21. Scott Sargrad, Khalilah M. Harris, Lisette Partelow, Neil Campbell, and Laura Jimenez, "A Quality Education for Every Child: A New Agenda for Education Policy," Center for American Progress, July 2, 2019, https://www.americanprogress.org/article/quality-education-every-child/.

22. Navtej Singh Johar & Others v. Union of India, Writ Petition (Criminal) No. 76 of 2016 (2018). United Nations, Universal Declaration of Human Rights, 1948, Article 26(2) emphasizes that "education shall be directed to the full development of the human personality." United Nations, International Covenant on Civil and Political Rights, 1966, Article 13(1) states that "parties . . . recognize the right of everyone to education [and] agree that education shall be directed to the full development of the human personality and the sense of its dignity, and shall strengthen the respect for human rights and fundamental freedoms." Taiwan Constitutional Court, Interpretation No. 603, Fingerprint Case, 2005; Peru Constitutional Tribunal, EXP. No. 02005-2009-PA/TC, Lima ONG, "Acción De Lucha Anticorrupción," paras. 5–6, 2009; Constitutional Court of Croatia, Decision U-I-60/1991, February 21, 2017, regarding abortion; Spain Constitutional Court, Judg-

ment STC 53/1985, April 11, 1985; Mexico Supreme Court, Acción de Inconstitucionalidad 2/2010 (Same-Sex Marriage and Adoption Case), 2010.

23. Spain, Constitution of Spain, Section 10.

24. Italy, Constitution of Italy, Article 3.

25. Mexico Supreme Court, Acción de Inconstitucionalidad 2/2010.

26. India Supreme Court, E. V. Chinnaiah v. State of Andhra Pradesh and Ors, November 5, 2004.

27. Canada, Canadian Charter of Rights and Freedoms, Section 15(2).

28. R. v. Kapp, 2008 SCC 41, [2008] 2 SCR 483, paras. 15 and 37, quoting Andrews v. Law Society of British Columbia, [1989] 1 SCR 143, 171.

29. *R. v. Kapp*, para. 38.

30. *R. v. Kapp*, paras. 80, 90, and 103, quoting R. v. Oakes, [1986] 1 SCR 103.

31. Constitutional Court of Colombia, Sentencia T-291/09 (Recyclers Case), 2009.

32. See, e.g., Indian Constitution; United Nations Human Rights Committee, General Comment No. 36 on Article 6 of the International Covenant on Civil and Political Rights.

33. Port Elizabeth Municipality v. Various Occupiers, [2004] ZACC 7, Constitutional Court of South Africa, October 1, 2004.

34. Constitutional Court of Germany, Judgment of May 4, 2011–2 BvR 2365/09, 2011.

35. Woodson v. North Carolina, 428 U.S. 280, 304 (1976), referring to the line from *Trop v. Dulles* about the dignity of men.

36. Miller v. Alabama, 567 U.S. 460, 489 (2012).

37. Mexican Supreme Court (2021), "Judgment on the Unconstitutionality of Abortion Laws in Coahuila and Sinaloa," para. 31.

38. Akdivar and Others v. Turkey, Application no. 21893/93, ECHR 1996-IV.

39. National Legal Services Authority v. Union of India and others, Writ Petition (Civil) No. 400 of 2012 (India 2014) at para. 20.

40. *National Legal Services Authority v. Union of India and others* at para. 67.

41. Port Elizabeth Municipality v. Various Occupiers, [2004] ZACC 7, Constitutional Court of South Africa, October 1, 2004.

42. "About: Students for Fair Admissions."

Chapter 3

1. In Mexico, where the population is more than 75 percent Catholic, the Court has adhered to the laicity of the state, "understood as the neutrality of the government before the pluralism of ideas and beliefs, whether religious or not, [which doesn't permit the state to] use state power to limit, define, or inhibit individual liberties that pertain to a person's convictions." Amparo en revisión 972/10, Suprema Corte de Justicia de la Nación (2011), para. 49.

2. Hodes & Nauser, MDs, P.A. v. Schmidt, 309 Kan. 610, 440 P.3d 461 (2019).

3. Eloise Barry, "The State of Abortion Rights Around the World," *Time*, May 3, 2022, https://time.com/6173229/countries-abortion-illegal-restrictions/#:~.

4. Amparo en revisión 267/2023 (La Primera Sala de la Suprema Corte de Justicia de la Nación), para. 43, citing Inter-American Court of Human Rights, Caso Artavia Murillo y otros ("Fecundación in vitro") vs. Costa Rica, Excepciones Preliminares, Fondo, Reparaciones y Costas, Sentencia de 28 de noviembre de 2012, Serie C No. 257, párr. 143.

5. In 2023, women made up 33 percent of state legislative bodies, up from 30 percent in 2022. "Women in State Legislatures for 2023," National Conference of State Legislatures, January 2023, https://www.ncsl.org/womens-legislative-network/women-in-state-legislatures-for-2023; and "Women in State Legislatures for 2022," National Council of State Legislatures, January 2022, https://www.ncsl.org/womens-legislative-network/women-in-state-legislatures-for-2022.

6. "After Roe Fell: Abortion Laws by State," Center for Reproductive Rights, accessed September 28, 2024, https://reproductiverights.org/maps/abortion-laws-by-state/.

7. Daniel Dench, Mayra Pineda-Torres, and Caitlin Knowles Myers, "The Effects of the Dobbs Decision on Fertility," November 15, 2023, https://ssrn.com/abstract=4634430.

8. Claire Cain Miller, "In Texas, Infant Mortality Rose after Abortion Ban," *New York Times*, June 26, 2024, https://www.nytimes.com/2024/06/26/upshot/texas-abortion-infant-mortality.html#:~.

9. Hodes & Nauser, MDs, P.A. v. Schmidt, 309 Kan. 610, 440 P.3d 461 (2019), https://cases.justia.com/kansas/supreme-court/2019-114153.pdf?ts=1556324975 at 45.

10. *Hodes & Nauser* at 74.

11. *Hodes & Nauser* at 74, 75.

12. Mariama Darame, "France, First to Protect Abortion in Its Consti-

tution, Sends Message to 'Women of the World,'" *Le Monde*, March 5, 2024, https://www.lemonde.fr/en/politics/article/2024/03/05/france -protecting-abortion-in-its-constitution-sends-message-to-women-of -the-world_6586538_5.html#:~; Joshua Berlinger and Xiaofei Xu, "France Becomes World's First Country to Enshrine Abortion Rights in Constitution," Yahoo News, March 5, 2024, https://www.yahoo.com/news/france -becomes-world-first-country-182016379.html?guccounter=2.

13. X v. The Principal Secretary, Health and Family Welfare Department, Govt. of NCT of Delhi & Anr., Civil Appeal No. 5802 of 2022 (Arising out of SLP [C] No. 12612 of 2022) (Supreme Court of India, September 2022), paras. 3 and 109.

14. Griswold v. Connecticut, 381 U.S. 479 (1965); Eisenstadt v. Baird, 405 U.S. 438 (1972); Roe v. Wade, 410 U.S. 113 (1973) (overruled); Planned Parenthood v. Casey, 505 U.S. 833 (1992) (overruled); Zablocki v. Redhail, 434 U.S. 374 (1978); Troxel v. Granville, 530 U.S. 57 (2000).

15. *X v. The Principal Secretary*, para. 109.

16. *X v. The Principal Secretary*, para. 110.

17. Amparo en revisión 267/2023, La Primera Sala de la Suprema Corte de Justicia de la Nación, 2023, para. 29.

18. *Amparo en revisión 267/2023*, para 35.

19. *Amparo en revisión 267/2023*, para. 38.

20. *Amparo en revisión 267/2023*, para. 48.

21. Dobbs v. Jackson Women's Health Organization, 597 U.S. ____, slip. op. at 52 (2022) (Breyer, Sotomayor, and Kagan, JJ., dissenting).

22. Corte IDH, Caso Artavia Murillo y otros (Fecundación in Vitro) vs. Costa Rica, Excepciones Preliminares, Fondo, Reparaciones y Costas, Sentencia de 28 de noviembre de 2012, Serie C No. 257, párr. 146; Comité para la Eliminación de la Discriminación contra la Mujer, Recomendación General No. 24 (La Mujer y la Salud), emitida el 02 de febrero de 1999, párr. 21 y 31, regarding CEDAW, Article 16.

23. Dobbs v. Jackson Women's Health Organization, 597 U.S. ____, slip. op. at 53 (2022) (Breyer, Sotomayor, and Kagan, JJ., dissenting).

24. Case of S.W. v. The United Kingdom (Application no. 20166/92) (European Court of Human Rights 1995).

25. Roni Caryn Rabin, "Religious Freedom Arguments Underpin Wave of Challenges to Abortion Bans," *New York Times*, June 28, 2023, https://www.nytimes.com/2023/06/28/health/abortion-religious-free dom.html.

26. Rachel Bayevsky, "Dignity and Judicial Authority," 2024, on file with the author.

Chapter 4

1. Anti-Defamation League, "You Will Not Replace Us," ADL, 2024, https://www.adl.org/resources/hate-symbol/you-will-not-replace-us.

2. Richard Fausset and Alan Blinder, "Heather Heyer, Charlottesville Victim, Is Recalled as 'a Strong Woman,'" *New York Times*, August 13, 2017, https://www.nytimes.com/2017/08/13/us/heather-heyer-charlottesville-victim.html.

3. Brandenburg v. Ohio, 395 U.S. 444 (1969).

4. Elonis v. United States, 575 U.S. 723 (2015).

5. Whitney v. California, 274 U.S. 357, 359–360 (1927).

6. Michael Rubikam and Julie Carr Smyth, "What to Know about the Threats in Springfield, Ohio, after False Claims about Haitian Immigrants," AP, September 22, 2024, https://apnews.com/article/springfield-ohio-haitian-immigrants-threats-key-details-7594bae869fb05dc6f106098409418cc.

7. Whitney v. California, 274 U.S. 357 (1927) (Brandeis, J., concurring).

8. Brandenburg v. Ohio, 395 U.S. 444 (1969).

9. Texas v. Johnson, 491 U.S. 397, 414 (1989).

10. West Virginia State Board of Education v. Barnette, 319 U.S. 624, 642 (1943).

11. R.A.V. v. City of St. Paul, 505 U.S. 377 (1992)

12. Chaplinsky v. New Hampshire, 315 U.S. 568, 572 (1942).

13. *Chaplinsky v. New Hampshire.*

14. R. v. Keegstra, [1990] 3 S.C.R. 697.

15. Criminal Code, R.S.C. 1985, c. C-46, s. 319(1) and (2) (Canada).

16. Criminal Code, s. 130(1) and (2).

17. Criminal Code, s. 130(3) and (4).

18. Constitution of Brazil, Chapter 1, Article 5, XLII.

19. "Teses do Supremo Tribunal Federal na ADO 26," Supremo Tribunal Federal, accessed September 22, 2024, https://www.stf.jus.br/arquivo/cms/noticiaNoticiaStf/anexo/tesesADO26.pdf.

20. Whitney v. California, 274 U.S. 357, 375 (1927) (Brandeis, J., concurring).

21. New York Times Co. v. Sullivan, 376 U.S. 254 (1964).

22. Cohen v. California, 403 U.S. 15, 24 (1971).

Chapter 5

1. Danielle Kaeble, "Probation and Parole in the United States, 2021," Bureau of Justice Statistics, February 2023, https://bjs.ojp.gov/

library/publications/probation-and-parole-united-states-2021#:~:text
=At%20yearend%202021%2C%20an%20estimated,the%20lowest%
20rate%20since%201987.

2. Kaeble, "Probation and Parole."

3. "Limiting Incarceration for Technical Violations of Probation and Parole," National Conference of State Legislatures, updated February 6, 2023, https://www.ncsl.org/civil-and-criminal-justice/limiting-in carceration-for-technical-violations-of-probation-and-parole#:~:text= On%20any%20given%20day%2C%20around,50%20states%20and% 20Washington%2C%20D.C.

4. "Following the Money of Mass Incarceration," Prison Policy Initiative, January 25, 2017, https://www.prisonpolicy.org/reports/money .html.

5. Tara O'Neill Hayes, "The Economic Costs of the U.S. Criminal Justice System," American Action Forum, July 16, 2020, https://www. americanactionforum.org/research/the-economic-costs-of-the-u-s -criminal-justice-system/.

6. Trop v. Dulles, 356 U.S. 86 (1958).

7. Brown v. Plata, 563 U.S. 493 (2011).

8. Neomi Rao, "Three Concepts of Dignity in Constitutional Law," *Notre Dame Law Review* 86 (2011): 183, 192.

9. Rao, "Three Concepts of Dignity," 183, 192.

10. Davis v. Neal, No. 1:21-cv-01773-TLA, 2023 U.S. Dist. LEXIS 144106 (D. Del. Aug. 17, 2023).

11. *Davis* at *23: "Cohen v. California, 403 U.S. 15, 24 (1971) (First Amendment protections are necessary to 'comport with the premise of individual dignity and choice upon which our political system rests'); Schmerber v. California, 384 U.S. 757 (1966), ('The overriding function of the Fourth Amendment is to protect personal privacy and dignity against unwarranted intrusion by the State'); Miranda v. Arizona, 384 U.S. 436, 460 (1966); Trop v. Dulles, 356 U.S. 86, 100 (1958) ('The basic concept underlying the Eighth Amendment is nothing less than the dignity of man'); Obergefell v. Hodges, 576 U.S. 644, 663 (2015) ('These liberties [protected by the Fourteenth Amendment] extend to certain personal choices central to individual dignity and autonomy'). In each of these cases, the Court mentioned dignity in connection with a claim for a violation of some other recognized right and not as the right itself."

12. See generally, Erin Daly, "Dignity in the Criminal Legal System," Delaware Law School Dignity Rights Clinic, 2024, https://delawarelaw .widener.edu/dignityclinic.

13. "Lists of Killings by Law Enforcement Officers in the United States," Wikiwand, accessed July 23, 2024, https://www.wikiwand.com/en/Lists_of_killings_by_law_enforcement_officers_in_the_United_States#Lists_of_killings.

14. "Mapping Police Violence," updated August 7, 2024, https://mappingpoliceviolence.org/.

15. "Mapping Police Violence."

16. "About Us," DefundPolice.org, 2021, https://defundpolice.org/about/. According to its website, "DefundPolice.org is coordinated, housed, and staffed by the Community Resource Hub. The project is a collaboration with Movement for Black Lives, Critical Resistance, Interrupting Criminalization, PolicyLink, Law for Black Lives, Database for Police Abolition, ACRE, Advancement Project, and Black Lives Matter Canada."

17. The Prison Policy Institute puts the number at 465,000. "Pretrial Detention," Prison Policy Initiative, accessed July 23, 2024, https://www.prisonpolicy.org/research/pretrial_detention/#:~:text=More%20than%20400%2C%20000%20people%20in,%22hold%22%20on%20their%20release. The Brennan Center for Justice puts the number at 536,000. "How Cash Bail Works," Brennan Center for Justice, February 24, 2021, https://www.brennancenter.org/our-work/research-reports/how-cash-bail-works.

18. "For Better or for Profit: How the Bail Bonding Industry Stands in the Way of Fair and Effective Pretrial Justice," Justice Policy Institute, September 2012, https://justicepolicy.org/wp-content/uploads/justicepolicy/documents/_for_better_or_for_profit_.pdf. However, due to the COVID-19 pandemic, many jurisdictions decreased the use of pretrial detention. See "COVID-19 Policy Response Survey," National Association of Pretrial Services Agencies, June 19, 2020, https://drive.google.com/file/d/1-jkFffQRmTTcqQoVOEJWlmyyJI--gExB/view.

19. Wendy Sawyer, "How Does Unaffordable Money Bail Affect Families?," Prison Policy Initiative, August 15, 2018, https://www.prisonpolicy.org/blog/2018/08/15/pretrial/; Tara O'Neill Hayes and Margaret Barnhorst, "Incarceration and Poverty in the United States," American Action Forum, June 30, 2020, https://www.americanactionforum.org/research/incarceration-and-poverty-in-the-united-states/. The numbers are 471,000 people are in jail without having been convicted of a crime while 161,000 have been convicted.

20. Sawyer, "How Does Unaffordable Money Bail Affect Families?"

21. Sawyer, "How Does Unaffordable Money Bail Affect Families?"

22. Sawyer, "How Does Unaffordable Money Bail Affect Families?"

23. Kaeble, "Probation and Parole."

24. Doris Layton Mackenzie, "Sentencing and Corrections in the 21st Century: Setting the Stage for the Future," Bureau of Justice Assistance, 2001, https://www.ojp.gov/sites/g/files/xyckuh241/files/archives/ncjrs/189106-2.pdf.

25. *Merriam-Webster Dictionary*, "Retribution," accessed July 24, 2024, https://www.merriam-webster.com/dictionary/retribution..

26. *Legal Dictionary*, "Specific Deterrence," August 12, 2017, https://legaldictionary.net/specific-deterrence/.

27. "Five Things about Deterrence," U.S. Department of Justice, National Institute of Justice, May 2016, https://www.ojp.gov/pdffiles1/nij/247350.pdf.

28. Gregg v. Georgia, 428 U.S. 153, 184–185 (1976).

29. Layton Mackenzie, "Sentencing and Corrections," *supra* note 365 at 9.

30. *Merriam-Webster Dictionary*, "Rehabilitation," accessed July 24, 2024, https://www.merriam-webster.com/dictionary/rehabilitation.

31. R. v. Bissonnette, [2022] S.C.C. 23 (Can.), *supra* note 22 at para. 83.

32. Ram Subramanian and Alison Shames, "Sentencing and Prison Practices in Germany and the Netherlands: Implications for the United States," Vera Institute of Justice, October 2013, https://www.vera.org/downloads/publications/european-american-prison-report-v3.pdf.

33. Subramanian and Shames, "Sentencing and Prison Practices," 7.

34. Subramanian and Shames, "Sentencing and Prison Practices," 7.

35. Subramanian and Shames, "Sentencing and Prison Practices," 8–9.

36. Subramanian and Shames, "Sentencing and Prison Practices," 13.

37. Layton Mackenzie, "Sentencing and Corrections," 12.

38. Layton Mackenzie, "Sentencing and Corrections," 18.

39. Layton Mackenzie, "Sentencing and Corrections," 19.

40. "Truth in Sentencing Law and Legal Definition," USLegal, accessed July 24, 2024, https://definitions.uslegal.com/t/truth-in-sentencing/.

41. Subramanian and Shames, "Sentencing and Prison Practices," 3.

42. Subramanian and Shames, "Sentencing and Prison Practices," 5.

43. Erin Daly, Paul Holdorf, Kelly Hartnett, Jane Doe, and Domo-

nique Grimes, "Women's Dignity, Women's Prisons: Combatting Sexual Abuse in America's Prisons," *CUNY Law Review* 26, no. 2 (2023): 262, 265–270.

44. "Dignity behind Bars," Vera Institute of Justice, accessed September 28, 2024, https://www.vera.org/dignity-behind-bars.

45. Walker v. State, 68 P.3d 872, 884 (Mont. 2003).

46. Montana Constitution, art. II, pt. 2, § 4.

47. *Davis v. Neal* at 16–17.

Chapter 6

1. This is why Justice Kennedy located dignity at the confluence of the equality and the liberty guarantees of the Fourteenth Amendment in *Obergefell v. Hodges*.

2. Matthew McManus, *Making Human Dignity Central to International Human Rights Law: A Critical Legal Argument* (Chicago: University of Chicago Press, 2020).

3. Jeremy Ney, "The Surprising Poverty Levels across the U.S.," *Time*, October 4, 2023, https://time.com/6320076/american-poverty -levels-state-by-state/.

4. Ney, "Surprising Poverty Levels," para. 2.

5. "2023 State of America's Children Report: Child Poverty," Children's Defense Fund, accessed September 28, 2024, https://www.chil drensdefense.org/tools-and-resources/the-state-of-americas-children/.

6. "Poverty Rate," OECD Data, accessed September 28, 2024, https: //data.oecd.org/inequality/poverty-rate.htm.

7. "Income Inequality and Fairness: A Deep Dive into Generational Wealth Gaps and Their Impact on the Economy," *Washington Post*, January 7, 2024, https://www.washingtonpost.com/opinions/2024/01/ 07/income-inequality-fairness-auten-splinter/.

8. "Telling the Nuanced Story of Economic Inequality in the U.S., Layer by Layer," Federal Reserve Bank of Minneapolis, 2023, https:// www.minneapolisfed.org/article/2023/telling-the-nuanced-story-of -economic-inequality-in-the-us-layer-by-layer.

9. Zia Qureshi, "Rising Inequality: A Major Issue of Our Time," Brookings Institution, May 16, 2023, https://www.brookings.edu/arti cles/rising-inequality-a-major-issue-of-our-time/.

10. World Inequality Lab, *World Inequality Report 2022*, European Commission Knowledge for Policy, 2022, para. 2, https://wir2022.wid .world/.

11. World Inequality Lab, *World Inequality Report 2022*.

12. "America's Poor Are Worse Off Than Elsewhere," Confronting Poverty, 2024, https://confrontingpoverty.org/poverty-facts-and -myths/americas-poor-are-worse-off-than-elsewhere/.

13. "America's Poor Are Worse Off Than Elsewhere."

14. "Child Tax Credit," Internal Revenue Service, updated August 20, 2024, https://www.irs.gov/credits-deductions/individuals/child -tax-credit.

15. "2023 State of America's Children Report."

16. Ney, "Surprising Poverty Levels."

17. Center on Budget and Policy Priorities, Statement of Sharon Parrott, CBPP President, on 2022 Census Poverty, Health, and Income Data, "Record Rise in Poverty Highlights Importance of Child Tax Credit; Health Coverage Marks a High Point before Pandemic Safeguards Ended," September 12, 2023, https://www.cbpp.org/press/ statements/record-rise-in-poverty-highlights-importance-of-child -tax-credit-health-coverage.

18. Parrrott, "Record Rise in Poverty."

19. Parrott, "Record Rise in Poverty."

20. In "The Playing Field Is Not Level," the Confronting Poverty investigation posits "a modified game of Monopoly, in which the players start out with quite different advantages and disadvantages, much as they do in life" and shows how generational inequalities as well as inequalities in neighborhoods, living conditions, educational opportunities, and so on affect the outcome. "Unfortunately," it reports, "the playing field in America is not level. Research has shown that the process begins with the financial resources of parents and the neighborhood a child is raised in. This then affects the quality of schooling a child receives, which then influences the type of job and career that they acquire and work at. All of these, in turn, can affect the quality of health an individual experiences, along with how well one is prepared for the retirement years." "The Playing Field Is Not Level," Confronting Poverty, accessed October 10, 2024, https://confrontingpoverty.org/ poverty-facts-and-myths/the-playing-field-is-not-level/.

21. Eduardo Porter, *American Poison: How Racial Hostility Destroyed Our Promise* (New York: Penguin Random House, 2021).

22. "General Comment 36 on the Interpretation of Article 6 of the International Covenant of Civil and Political Rights," accessed September 24, 2024, https://www.ohchr.org/sites/default/files/Documents /HRBodies/CCPR/GCArticle6/GCArticle6_EN.pdf.

23. "General Comment 36," para. 3.

24. "General Comment 36," para. 26.

25. "General Comment 36," para. 26.

26. *"Hartz IV Decision,"* BVerfG, 1 BvL 1/09, Federal Constitutional Court, Germany, February 9, 2010.

27. *"Recyclers Case,"* Sentencia T-291/09, Constitutional Court of Colombia, 2009.

28. American Bar Association, "Resolution 113B," August 2019, *supra* note 4.

29. Austin Clemens, Shanteal Lake, and David S. Mitchell, "Evidence from the 2020 Election Shows How to Close the Income Voting Divide," Washington Center for Equitable Growth, July 28, 2021, https://equitablegrowth.org/evidence-from-the-2020-election-shows-how-to-close-the-income-voting-divide/.

30. *"Hartz IV Decision."*

31. *"Mohini Jain v. State of Karnataka,"* AIR 1992 SC 1858, para. 67, quoting "Francis Coralie Mullin v. Union Territory of Delhi," AIR 1981 SC 746.

Chapter 7

1. Samantha Allen, "30% Of Americans Cite Climate Change as a Motivator to Move in 2024," Forbes Home, January 5, 2024, https://www.forbes.com/home-improvement/features/americans-moving-climate-change/.

2. Bella Isaacs-Thomas, "Climate Change Is Hitting Close to Home for Nearly 2 out of 3 Americans, Poll Finds," PBS News Hour, August 3, 2023, https://www.pbs.org/newshour/science/climate-change-is-hitting-close-to-home-for-nearly-2-out-of-3-americans-poll-finds.

3. "The Impact of Climate Change on American Household Finances," U.S. Department of the Treasury, September 2023, 1, https://home.treasury.gov/system/files/136/Climate_Change_Household_Finances.pdf.

4. Greg Iacurci, "Many Americans Think They're Insulated from Climate Change. Their Finances Indicate Otherwise," CNBC, July 16, 2024, https://www.cnbc.com/2024/07/16/how-climate-change-may-impact-americans-wallets.html.

5. Evan Bush, "On One Night, Two Places in the Northeast Get Hit with 1-in-1,000 Year Rainfall," NBC News, August 19, 2024, https://www.nbcnews.com/science/environment/northeast-two-instances-1-in-1000-year-rainfall-rcna167204.

6. Li Cohen, "Here's How Hurricane Helene Brought 'Biblical Dev-

astation' to Western North Carolina in a Near 'Worst-Case Scenario,'" CBS News, October 1, 2024, https://www.cbsnews.com/news/hurri cane-helene-biblical-devastation-north-carolina-near-worst-case-sce nario/; Simon Ducroquet, John Muyskens, Naema Ahmed, Nicolás Rivero, and Niko Kommenda, "How Helene Became a 'Worst Case Scenario,'" *Washington Post*, accessed October 8, 2024, https://www.wash ingtonpost.com/climate-environment/interactive/2024/helene-flood ing-damage-north-carolina-chimney-rock/?itid=hp-top-table-main_ p001_f004&utm_campaign=wp_post_most&utm_medium=email& utm_source=newsletter&wpisrc=nl_most&carta-url=https%3A%2F %2Fs2.washingtonpost.com%2Fcar-ln-tr%2F3f34ea9%2F67015c3839 cb8c5d208a4c83%2F5983b45b9bbcof6826e2fe01%2F13%2F48%2F67 015c3839cb8c5d208a4c83; "Hurricane Helene Damages Could Hit $35 Billion," Axios, October 1, 2024, https://www.axios.com/2024/10/01/ hurricane-helene-damages-35-billion; John Yang, Andrew Corkery, and Claire Mufson, "Helene's Destruction Puts Spotlight on Costly Gaps in Homeowners Insurance," PBS News Weekend, October 6, 2024, https://www.pbs.org/newshour/show/helenes-destruction-puts -spotlight-on-costly-gaps-in-homeowners-insurance.

7. Jonathan Belles, Chris Dolce, Caitlin Kaiser, and Sara Tonks, "Milton Expected to Bring Potentially Life Threatening and Destructive Storm Surge, Winds, Flooding Rain to Florida," Weather Channel, October 8, 2024, https://weather.com/storms/hurricane/news/2024-10 -08-hurricane-milton-florida-forecast-storm-surge-wind-damage -rainfall; "Live Updates: Milton Regains Category 5 Strength as It Plows toward Tampa," *New York Times*, October 8, 2024, https://www .nytimes.com/live/2024/10/08/weather/hurricane-milton-florida.

8. "Ron DeSantis Signs Bill Scrubbing 'Climate Change' from Florida State Laws," *The Guardian*, May 16, 2024, https://www.theguardian .com/us-news/article/2024/may/16/desantis-climate-change-energy -bill.

9. "Impact of Climate Change."

10. "Impact of Climate Change," 1.

11. United States Global Change Research Program, "Fifth National Climate Assessment," https://nca2023.globalchange.gov/.

12. United States Global Change Research Program, "Fifth National Climate Assessment."

13. "United States Strategy to Respond to the Effects of Climate Change on Women 2023," US Department of State, 2023, https://www

.state.gov/reports/united-states-strategy-to-respond-to-the-effects-of -climate-change-on-women-2023/.

14. United States Global Change Research Program, "Fifth National Climate Assessment."

15. United States Global Change Research Program, "Fifth National Climate Assessment."

16. Samantha Montano, "America's Disaster Recovery System Is a Disaster," *New York Times*, October 28, 2023, https://www.nytimes .com/2023/10/28/opinion/fema-aid-disaster-recovery-climate-change .html.

17. Mario Alejandro Ariza, "Miami Is Entering a State of Unreality: No Amount of Adaptation to Climate Change Can Fix Miami's Water Problems," *The Atlantic*, June 18, 2024. https://www.theatlantic.com/ science/archive/2024/06/miami-climate-change-floods/678718/.

18. Scott Dance, " 'Not Prepared': Why the Midwest Floods Are a Warning for the Nation," *Washington Post*, June 29, 2024, https://www .washingtonpost.com/weather/2024/06/29/rapidan-dam-floods-ex treme-rains-infrastructure/.

19. Dennis Brady and Chris Mooney, "The New Face of Flooding," *Washington Post*, July 15, 2024, https://www.washingtonpost.com/ climate-environment/interactive/2024/flooding-sea-level-rise-gulf -coast/.

20. Brady and Mooney, "The New Face of Flooding," para. 8.

21. Brady Dennis, Kevin Crowe, and John Muyskens, "A Hidden Threat: Fast-Rising Seas Could Swamp Septic Systems in Parts of the South," *Washington Post*, May 22, 2024, https://www.washingtonpost .com/climate-environment/interactive/2024/septic-tanks-rising -waters-environment-health/?itid=ap_bradydennis.

22. Lunna Lopes, Alex Montero, Marley Presiado, and Liz Hamel, "Americans' Challenges with Health Care Costs," March 1, 2024, https: //www.kff.org/health-costs/issue-brief/americans-challenges-with -health-care-costs/.

23. Lopes et al., "Americans' Challenges."

24. Megan Brenan, "Majority in U.S. Still Say Gov't Should Ensure Healthcare," Gallup, January 23, 2023, https://news.gallup.com/poll/ 468401/majority-say-gov-ensure-healthcare.aspx.

25. "Countries with Single Payer 2024," World Population Review, January 2024, https://worldpopulationreview.com/country-rankings/ countries-with-single-payer. "As of January 2024, the following coun-

tries operated single-payer health-care solutions: Australia, Bahrain, Bhutan, Botswana, Brazil, Brunei, Canada, Cuba, Denmark, Finland, France, Georgia, Greece, Hong Kong, Iceland, Italy, Kuwait, Macau, Malaysia, Maldives, Malta, New Zealand, North Korea, Norway, Oman, Portugal, San Marino, Saudi Arabia, South Africa, South Korea, Spain, Sri Lanka, Sweden, Taiwan, Trinidad and Tobago, Ukraine, and United Kingdom."

26. Bradley Jones, "Increasing Share of Americans Favor a Single Government Program to Provide Health Care Coverage," Pew Research Center, September 29, 2020, https://www.pewresearch.org/short-reads/2020/09/29/increasing-share-of-americans-favor-a-single-government-program-to-provide-health-care-coverage/.

27. Joe Murphy, "Map: Flood Insurance Coverage Lowest in Counties Hit Hardest by Helene," NBC News, October 3, 2024, https://www.nbcnews.com/data-graphics/map-flood-insurance-coverage-counties-hit-hurricane-helene-rcna173619.

28. Chris Mooney, "Why Americans Pay So Much More Than Anyone Else for Weather Disasters," *Washington Post*, March 16, 2024, https://www.washingtonpost.com/climate-environment/2024/03/16/us-disaster-costs-second-world/.

29. "FEMA," Federal Emergency Management Agency, accessed July 24, 2024, https://www.fema.gov/.

30. Montano, "America's Disaster Recovery System."

31. Montano, "America's Disaster Recovery System."

32. Montano, "America's Disaster Recovery System."

33. Montano, "America's Disaster Recovery System."

34. Alec Tyson and Brian Kennedy, "Two-Thirds of Americans Think Government Should Do More on Climate," Pew Research Center, June 23, 2020, https://www.pewresearch.org/science/2020/06/23/two-thirds-of-americans-think-government-should-do-more-on-climate/.

35. This includes 95 percent of liberal Democrats, 86 percent of moderate/conservative Democrats, and 46 percent of liberal/moderate Republicans, but only 13 percent of conservative Republicans.

36. Alec Tyson, Cary Funk, and Brian Kennedy, "What the Data Says about Americans' Views of Climate Change," Pew Research Center, August 9, 2023, https://www.pewresearch.org/short-reads/2023/08/09/what-the-data-says-about-americans-views-of-climate-change/.

37. Joshua Glanzer, "Floridians Believe in Climate Change and Want

Government Action," Florida Atlantic University Newsdesk, October 23, 2023, https://www.fau.edu/newsdesk/articles/oct23climatesurvey.

38. See Los Angeles County Flood Control District v. Natural Resources Defense Council, 568 U.S. 78 (2013) (limiting EPA's authority under the Clean Water Act); Utility Air Regulatory Group v. EPA, 573 U.S. 302 (2014) (limiting EPA's authority under the Clean Air Act to treat greenhouse gases as a pollutant for certain purposes); Michigan v. Envtl. Prot. Agency, 576 U.S. 743 (2015) (requiring EPA to consider corporate costs in the decision whether to regulate power plants).

39. West Virginia v. EPA, 597 U.S. 697 (2022).

40. "Supreme Court Catastrophically Undermines Clean Water Protections," Earthjustice, May 25, 2023, https://earthjustice.org/brief/2023/supreme-court-sackett-clean-water-act (noting that "more than half of the 118 million acres of wetlands in the United States are threatened by this ruling").

41. Jeff Turrentine, "What the Supreme Court's Sackett v. EPA Ruling Means for Wetlands and Other Waterways," National Resources Defense Council, June 5, 2023, https://www.nrdc.org/stories/what-you-need-know-about-sackett-v-epa.

42. Ohio v. Env't Prot. Agency, No. 23A349, 2024 WL 3187768 at *11 (U.S. June 27, 2024) (Barrett J., dissenting).

43. Loper Bright Enterprises v. Raimondo, No. 22–1219, 2024 WL 3208360 at *5 (U.S. June 28, 2024).

44. Juliana v. United States, No. 18–36082 (9th Cir. 2020) at 11.

45. *Juliana v. United States* at 14–15.

46. *Juliana v. United States* at 15–16.

47. *Juliana v. United States* at 19–21.

48. *Juliana v. United States* at 20.

49. United States v. District Court for the District of Oregon, May 1, 2024.

50. *Juliana v. United States* at 31–32.

51. R (on the application of Finch on behalf of the Weald Action Group) (Appellant) v. Surrey County Council and others (Respondents), Case ID: 2022/0064, June 20, 2024.

52. Obergefell v. Hodges, 576 U.S. 644 (2015).

53. United States v. Lopez, 514 U.S. 549 (1995).

54. As the Supreme Court explained the gun case, "We start with first principles. The Constitution creates a Federal Government of enumerated powers. See Art. i, § 8. As James Madison wrote: 'The powers

delegated by the proposed Constitution to the federal government are few and defined. Those which are to remain in the State governments are numerous and indefinite.' The Federalist No. 45, pp. 292–293 (C. Rossiter ed. 1961). . . . The Constitution . . . withhold[s] from Congress a plenary police power that would authorize enactment of every type of legislation. See Art. i, § 8." *United States v. Lopez.*

55. Patient Protection and Affordable Care Act of 2010, Pub. L. No. 111–148, 124 Stat. 119 (2010).

56. American Rescue Plan Act of 2021, H.R. 1319, 117th Cong. (2021), https://www.congress.gov/bill/117th-congress/house-bill/1319/text.

57. Infrastructure Investment and Jobs Act, H.R. 3684, 117th Cong. (2021), https://www.congress.gov/bill/117th-congress/house-bill/3684.

58. "Treasury Announces Guideline on Inflation Reduction Act's Strong Labor Protections," U.S. Department of the Treasury, November 29, 2022, https://home.treasury.gov/news/press-releases/jy1128.

59. Christina DeConcini, Jennifer Rennicks, and Shannon Wood, "One Year In, How the Inflation Reduction Act Is Creating a Manufacturing Resurgence in the US," August 9, 2023, https://www.wri.org/insights/inflation-reduction-act-anniversary-manufacturing-resurgence. See also "US Inflation Reduction Act: A Catalyst for Climate Action," Credit Suisse, November 30, 2022, https://www.credit-suisse.com/about-us-news/en/articles/news-and-expertise/us-inflation-reduction-act-a-catalyst-for-climate-action-202211.html: "Credit Suisse estimates total federal spending at double the headline figure—to over USD 800 billion—sending the total public and private spending mobilized by the IRA to nearly USD 1.7 trillion over the next ten years."

60. See "US Inflation Reduction Act": "The public spending will likely trigger private sector investment (i.e. the 'leverage effect'). The multiplier generally ranges from 1.1x to 1.6x2, meaning for every dollar of public spending, at least 1.1 dollar would be spent by the private sector. Subsidized lending from the Department of Energy's loan program and Greenhouse Gas Reduction Fund (i.e. green banks) will supercharge green financing."

61. "Inflation Reduction Act of 2022: Climate and Energy Provisions," ERM, October 2022, https://www.erm.com/globalassets/documents/insights/2022/issue-brief-ira-climate-2022-climate-energy-provisions.pdf.

62. "Under a business-as-usual scenario (without the IRA), the U.S. would be expected to reduce greenhouse gas (GHG) emissions by between 24% and 35% by 2030 compared to 2005 levels. This reduction is

a far cry from the 50–52% reduction target set in the latest U.S. nationally determined contribution (NDC). With the passage of the IRA, GHG reductions are expected to reach 31% to 44% by 2030. When combined with renewed ambition from executive agencies like the EPA and Department of Agriculture, as well as states and cities, the Rhodium Group's modeling suggests that the U.S. can meet its NDC commitment." Melissa Barbanell, "A Brief Summary of the Climate and Energy Provisions of the Inflation Reduction Act of 2022," World Resources Institute, October 28, 2022, https://www.wri.org/update/brief-summary-climate-and-energy-provisions-inflation-reduction-act-2022.

63. Michael Stavish, Gabe Rubio, and Lisa Kieth, "ESG and the Inflation Reduction Act of 2022," BDO USA, October 2022, https://www.bdo.com/insights/tax/esg-and-the-inflation-reduction-act-of-2022.

64. "Multiple independent analyses show the bill will reduce U.S. greenhouse gas emissions some 40% below 2005 levels by 2030, a big step toward President Biden's goal of cutting them in half by 2030." Fred Krupp, "The Biggest Thing Congress Has Ever Done to Address Climate Change," Environmental Defense Fund, August 12, 2022, https://www.edf.org/blog/2022/08/12/biggest-thing-congress-has-ever-done-address-climate-change.

65. Laura Feiveson and Matthew Ashenfarb, "The Inflation Reduction Act: Saving American Households Money While Reducing Climate Change and Air Pollution," U.S. Department of the Treasury, August 7, 2024, https://home.treasury.gov/news/featured-stories/the-inflation-reduction-act-saving-american-households-money-while-reducing-climate-change-and-air-pollution.

66. Bobby Kogan and Brendan Kirk, "The Inflation Reduction Act Still Reduces the Deficit," Center for American Progress, June 27, 2024, https://www.americanprogress.org/article/the-inflation-reduction-act-still-reduces-the-deficit/.

67. Anthony Leiserowitz, Edward Maibach, Seth Rosenthal, John Kotcher, Emily Goddard, Jennifer Carman, Marija Verner, et al., *Climate Change in the American Mind: Politics and Policy, Fall 2023*, noting that "a majority of registered voters (58%) have heard at least 'a little' about the Inflation Reduction Act of 2022, but only 36% have heard either 'a lot' (12%) or 'some' (24%) about it. Liberal Democrats (43%) and conservative Republicans (42%) are the most likely to have heard 'a lot' or 'some' about the IRA, while fewer moderate/conservative Democrats (31%) or liberal/moderate Republicans (23%) have. About four in ten registered voters (41%) have heard 'nothing at all'

about the IRA." See https://climatecommunication.yale.edu/publica
tions/climate-change-in-the-american-mind-politics-policy-fall-2023
or https://climatecommunication.yale.edu/publications/climate
-change-in-the-american-mind-politics-policy-fall-2023/toc/7/.

Chapter 8

1. In 1824, Andrew Jackson won the popular vote by about 10 percentage points, but the House of Representatives gave the election to
John Quincy Adams; in 1876, Samuel Tilden received a majority of
votes (not just a plurality), but in a deal that would have monumental
consequences to this day because it ended Reconstruction, Republican
Rutherford B. Hayes became president; in 1888, Grover Cleveland won
slightly more votes than Republican president Benjamin Harrison; in
2000, Al Gore won slightly more votes than Republican president
George W. Bush in a contested election decided by the Supreme Court;
and in 2016, Hillary Clinton won the popular vote by 2 percentage
points, but Republican Donald Trump became president.

2. "Voting Rights Laws and Constitutional Amendments," USA.gov,
accessed July 24, 2024, https://www.usa.gov/voting-rights.

3. South Carolina v. Katzenbach, 383 U.S. 301, 308 (1966).

4. Shelby County v. Holder, 570 U.S. 529 (2013).

5. *Shelby County v. Holder*, quoting from 152 *Cong. Rec.* S8781 (Aug.
3, 2006).

6. Liz Avore, "10 Years since Shelby v. Holder: Where We Are and
Where We're Heading," Voting Rights Lab, June 27, 2023, https://vo
tingrightslab.org/2023/06/27/10-years-since-shelby-v-holder-where
-we-are-and-where-were-heading/.

7. Avore, "10 Years Since Shelby v. Holder."

8. Avore, "10 Years Since Shelby v. Holder."

9. South Africa Const., Art. 19 (3) (a).

10. August and Another v. Electoral Commission and Others
(CCT8/99) [1999] ZACC 3.

11. Matatiele Municipality and Others v. President of the Republic of
South Africa and Others, Case CCT 73/05 (2006) (J. Ngcobo), para. 66.

12. *August and Another v. Electoral Commission and Others.*

13. *August and Another v. Electoral Commission and Others.*

14. Arshad Mehmood v. The Commissioner of Elections in Pakistan,
High Court, Case No: W.P. No. 31986/2013.

15. Whitney v. California, 274 U.S. 357, 375 (1927) (Brandeis, J. diss.).

16. *Arshad Mehmood v. The Commissioner of Elections in Pakistan.*

17. Lisbon Case, BVerfG, 2 BvE 2/08, vom 30.6.2009, para. 211.

18. Bundesrat v. National Democratic Party of Germany, 2 BvB 1/13 (2017) at 541.

19. *Bundesrat v. National Democratic Party of Germany* at 538.

20. *Bundesrat v. National Democratic Party of Germany* at 541.

21. *Bundesrat v. National Democratic Party of Germany* at 586.

22. Cohen v. California, 403 U.S. 15 (1971).

23. "Election Day," Wikiwand, accessed July 24, 2024, https://www .wikiwand.com/en/Election_day.

24. M. Keith Chen, Kareem Haggag, Devin G. Pope, and Ryne Rohla, "Racial Disparities in Voting Wait Times: Evidence from Smartphone Data," National Bureau of Economic Research, November 2020, https://www.nber.org/papers/w26487.

25. "Common Voting Restrictions Are More Harmful Than You Might Think," League of Women Voters, July 29, 2023, https://www. lwv.org/blog/common-voting-restrictions-are-more-harmful-you -might-think.

26. Christopher Uggen, Ryan Larson, Sarah Shannon, and Robert Stewart, "Locked Out 2022: Estimates of People Denied Voting Rights," The Sentencing Project, October 25, 2022, https://www.sentencingpro ject.org/reports/locked-out-2022-estimates-of-people-denied-voting -rights/.

Epilogue

1. American Bar Association, "Resolution 113B," adopted August 2019, *supra* note 4.

2. Ackermann, *Human Dignity*.

Bibliographic Essay

First, let me confess that I have not read all or even most of the books mentioned in the notes below. One simply could not. By the half point of 2024, there were approximately one hundred books available on Amazon with 2024 publication dates with "dignity" in the title. HeinOnline counts nearly two thousand articles with "dignity" in the title in its database of law journals.

Some are legal, some are religious, some are personal memoirs and self-help books, some are about beauty (both inside and out), and some are fictional, but most are not. Some are about interpersonal relationships, and others soar into the abstract realms of international human rights law and spiritual journeys. Some, like Mark Coleman's *The Dignity Doctrine: Rational Relations in an Irrational World*, somehow lie at the intersection of both:

> Anything and everything about your life has a purpose. You evoke your purpose when and how you choose to be a part of change. Therein lies dignity. We live our life's highest purpose when we freely and openly choose to be ourselves, ready for action, ready for change, ready for service. . . . What you, I, and we need right now

> . . . is a world that is ready to roll up its sleeves, one that gets off the sofa and tells a world that is increasingly irrational that we need to recalibrate entrenched relationships, challenge convention, and redefine what it means to be human."[a]

Surveying dignity titles over the last few years, we see books and articles that coalesce around certain broad themes. I will describe some of these briefly and then focus on some of the areas that seem most relevant to this book. Many of these works straddle different groupings, and I have done my best to place them appropriately, though I am sure there is room for quibbling about which category describes them best.

First, there are a number of dignity titles that are personal memoirs, often about surviving a particular form of trauma, often a medical one. These books are interesting because they suggest a particular form of the concept of dignity—the idea that dignity connotes a kind of integrity, and if you can survive Parkinson's or cancer, or divorce for that matter, with dignity, then you have emerged with the essence of your being intact. This is both a matter of personal pride and the ability to maintain the respect of others.[b] For the end of this journey, there are a large

---

[a] Mark Coleman, *The Dignity Doctrine: Rational Relations in an Irrational World* (2020).

[b] Joni J. Seith, *The Pain of Grace: Living and Suffering with Dignity* (2024); Donna Shin-Ward, *My Mystical Path: A Memoir of Finding Grace and Dignity in Life's Hardest Lessons* (2023); Martine Le Corre, *Mine Are My Strength* (2023); Varoujan Der Simonian and Sophia Mekhitarian, *The Dignity of Being Armenian* (2023); Heike Thieme, *Company in the Moon: Dignity—Trust—Wonder* (2022); J. N. Blackwood, *Dignity: A True Story* (2022); Yonah 'Imanu'el and Shmuel Emanuel, *Dignity to Survive: One Family's Story of Faith in the Holocaust* (2022); Terri Pease, *Love, Dignity & Parkinson's: From Care Partner to Caregiver* (2022).

number of books about death with dignity, which connotes an entirely different aspect of dignity—the part of dignity that demands control over how one lives one's life, all the way to the end. The "death with dignity language" conveys this sense of autonomy and control: we each get to decide for ourselves how and when we will end our lives.[c] There are a few books about aging with dignity, which seem to be both about personal pride and respect and maintaining agency.[d]

Then, there are books that use the idea of respect as the touchstone of professional life, spanning everything from do-

---

[c] Books about death with dignity include Jonathan Denis, *Dying with Dignity: Advocacy for the Last of Freedoms* (2024); Emmanuel Hirsch, *Duty to Die, Dignified and Free* (2023); Sylvia Poss, *Towards Death with Dignity: Caring for Dying People* (2022); Derya Nur Kayacan, *The Right to Die with Dignity: How Far Do Human Rights Extend?* (2022); Sean Davison, *The Price of Mercy: A Fight for Your Right to Die with Dignity* (2022); Alison Clay-Duboff, *Living with Veracity, Dying with Dignity* (2022); Laure Delarche, *Dying with Dignity: A Qualitative Study on the Opinions of Home Care Actors in Lot-et-Garonne* (2021); Gilles Pornin, Robert William Higgins, Jacques Ricot, Patrick Baudry, and Elisabeth Maillaud, *The Dying: The Status of the Dying, the Dignity of the Dying, the Place of the Dying* (2020); Jean Liberté, *Manifesto for a Right to Painless Suicide: A Pro-Choice Essay on Human Dignity* (2019); Jeffrey A. Brauch, "Preserving True Human Dignity in Human Rights Law," *Capital University Law Review* 50 (2022): 115; Nathan T. Levy, "Death with Dignity: Terminally Ill(inois)," *Southern Illinois University Law Journal* 46 (2022): 321; Maeve O'Rourke, *Human Rights and the Care of Older People: Dignity, Vulnerability, and the Anti-torture Norm* (2024); Gilles Berrut, *Aging with Dignity: The Obvious Challenge* (2022).

[d] Maeve O'Rourke, *Human Rights and the Care of Older People: Dignity, Vulnerability, and the Anti-torture Norm* (2024); Gilles Berrut, *Aging with Dignity: The Obvious Challenge* (2022).

mestic work to development work, and including medicine, architecture, education, sex work, and social service. These often focus on dignity as a metonym for respect, in the sense of treating a person as a person, not as an object. Some argue that the professions should treat others with respect, while other books argue that we should treat the professionals with respect.[e]

---

[e] Dignity books about work and professional life include Christa Teston, *Doing Dignity: Ethical Praxis and the Politics of Care* (2024); Cait Lamberton, Neela A. Saldanha, and Tom Wein, *Marketplace Dignity: Transforming How We Engage with Customers across Their Journey* (2024) [customer care]; Peter Becker, *Leading with Heart: How You as a Versatile Leader Can Successfully Lead with Dignity, Values, and Trust in a Digital Working World 4.0* (2024); Jérôme Kouadio, *Dignity of the Human Cadaver in a Medico-Legal Context During CoViD-19* (2023) [funeral services]; Harvey Max Chochinov, *Dignity in Care: The Human Side of Healthcare* (2023); Myriam Sylvie Ambomo, *Nursing Practice and Human Dignity* (2022); Eoin Ó Broin and Mal McCann, *Dignity of Everyday Life: Celebrating Michael Scott's Busáras* (2022) [architecture]; Angie Freese, *Meant for More: Real Talk about Classrooms Built on Dignity, Authenticity, and Connection* (2023) [overcoming educational inequity]; Tamar Ketko, Hana Bor, and Khalid Arar, *Enhancing Values of Dignity, Democracy, and Diversity in Higher Education: Comparative Insights for Challenging Times* (2022) [education]; Decoteau J. Irby, Charity Anderson, and Charles M. Payn, *Dignity-Affirming Education: Cultivating the Somebodiness of Students and Educators* (2022); Ann P. Turnbull, Michael L. Wehmeyer, Karrie Ann Shogren, Meghan M. Burke, and H. Rutherford Turnbull, *Exceptional Lives: Practice, Progress, & Dignity in Today's Schools* (2024); Jana Costas, *Dramas of Dignity: Cleaners in the Corporate Underworld of Berlin* (2022) [office cleaners]; Zeynep Ton, *Case for Good Jobs: How Great Companies Bring Dignity, Pay & Meaning to Everyone's Work* (2022); Tom G. Palmer and Matt Warner, *Development with Dignity: Self-Determination, Localization, and the End to Poverty* (2022) [development work]; Paolo G. Carozza, *The Practice of Human Development and Dignity* (2020); Stewart Cunningham,

There are also a number of books that bring the concept of dignity to histories and geographies, from the Greco-Roman world to the Shoah to Afghanistan to Ukraine.[f] Some of these

---

Sex Work and Human Dignity: Law, Politics, and Discourse (2022); Harvey Max Chochinov, *Dignity in Care: The Human Side of Medicine* (2022); Arindrajit Dube, Suresh Naidu, and Adam D. Reich, *Power and Dignity in the Low-Wage Labor Market: Theory and Evidence from Wal-Mart Workers* (2022); Stephen G. Post and Jade C. Angelica, *Dignity for Deeply Forgetful People: How Caregivers Can Meet the Challenges of Alzheimer's Disease* (2022); Gladys Trézenem, *Human Dignity and the Administrative Judge* (2021); Léon Germe, *On Dignity and Quackery in Medicine* (2021); Fatié Ouattara, *Educating Is Humanizing: Dignity, Integrity, Secularity, and Violence* (2020) [education]; Erynn Masi de Casanova, *Dust and Dignity: Domestic Employment in Contemporary Ecuador* (2019); Frank M. McClellan, *Healthcare and Human Dignity: Law Matters* (2019); Vincent Gay, *For Dignity: Immigrant Workers and Social Conflicts in the 1980s* (2021); Baowendsida Noël Nana, *Diplomacy in Service of Human Dignity* (2020); Mark Erlich, *The Way We Build: Restoring Dignity to Construction Work* (2023); Ludmila N. Praslova, *The Canary Code: A Guide to Neurodiversity, Dignity, and Intersectional Belonging at Work* (2024) [building neurodiverse workplaces].

There is some law review commentary on Michael Sandel's work about work, including Daniel Hemel, "Beyond the Dignity of Work: Comment on M. Sandel's *The Tyranny of Merit*," *American Journal of Law and Equality* 1 (2021): 33. Other articles about dignity and work include Bridget Nicole Gonzalez, "Employment Classification and Human Dignity in the Gig Economy," *St. Thomas Law Review* 34 (2021): 52 [assessing whether human dignity is taken into account in legislative and judicial decision-making regarding worker classification since human dignity should be at the core of all work environments]; Lynn D. Lu, "From Stigma to Dignity? Transforming Workfare with Universal Basic Income and a Federal Job Guarantee," *South Carolina Law Review* 72 (2021): 703.

[f] Histories and geographies with dignity include Léon Sann, *The Shoah and the Limits of Dignity: A Study at the Intersection of Decency and*

take the form of individual biographies;[g] others address broader issues, usually in the context of some kind of justice.[h] Christa Bruhn's *Crossing Borders: The Search for Dignity in Palestine: A Memoir* is a notable example of this genre, both personal and political and particularly salient these days.[i]

Incarnation (2024); Marie Augier, Christophe Badel, and Jean-Luc Bastien, *Honor and Dignity in the Ancient World* (2023); Emmanuelle Gindre, *The Dignity of Detained Persons in Overseas Prisons* (2023); Giovanni Ercolani and Chris Farrands, *The Maidan Museum: Art, Identity, and the Revolution of Dignity* (2023); Kalman Mizsei, *Eight Years after the Revolution of Dignity: What Has Changed in Ukraine during 2013–2021?* (2022); Florian Weigand, *Waiting for Dignity: Legitimacy and Authority in Afghanistan* (2022); Christopher Courtheyn, *Community of Peace: Performing Geographies of Ecological Dignity in Colombia* (2022); Hélène Becquet and Bettina Frederking, *The Dignity of Kings: Perspectives on Royalty in France in the Early 19th Century* (2019); Miguel Pérez, *The Right to Dignity: Housing Struggles, City Making, and Citizenship in Urban Chile* (2022); Zaynab El Bernoussi, *Dignity in the Egyptian Revolution: Protest and Demand during the Arab Uprisings* (2021).

[g] Works about people who lived with dignity include Sarojini Nadar, *Ecumenical Encounters with Desmond Mpilo Tutu: Visions for Justice, Dignity and Peace* (2022); Janet Benge and Geoff Benge, *Frederick Douglass: The Right to Dignity* (2022); Russell J. Levenson, *Witness to Dignity: The Life and Faith of George H. W. and Barbara Bush* (2022); Eugen Brand and Michel Sauquet, *Dignity as Compass* (2020); Donatella Pagliacci, *Human Dignity and Moral Life: The Way of Augustine* (2020); Karen Ellis, *Fannie Lou Hamer: The Courageous Woman Who Marched for Dignity* (2023).

[h] Examples of these are David Buckham, Robyn Wilkinson, and Christiaan Straeuli, *The Age of Menace: Capitalism, Inequality & the Battle for Dignity* (2022); Kimberly Ivette Miranda, *Dignity and Rebellion in the Barrio: Housing Justice Organizing in Los Angeles' Eastside* (2024).

[i] Christa Bruhn, *Crossing Borders: The Search for Dignity in Palestine: A Memoir* (2023).

More broadly still are the books that look at dignity as the touchstone of a religious inquiry,[j] and others look at dignity as the touchstone of a philosophical inquiry.[k]

---

[j] Books focusing on dignity from a religious perspective include Nadya Williams, *Mothers, Children, and the Body Politic: Ancient Christianity and the Recovery of Human Dignity* (2024); Amy Schisler, *Clothed with Strength and Dignity: Women of the Bible* (2023); Sara Contini, *Human Dignity in the Latin Reception of Origen* (2023); *Christian Perspectives on Human Dignity and Human Rights from a Peace Church Perspective* [Church of the Brethren] (2022); George Hickes, *Two Treatises, One of the Christian Priesthood, the Other of the Dignity of the Episcopal Order* (2022); Prove Peter, Motte Jochen, Dressler Sabine, and Parlindugan Andar, *Strengthening Christian Perspectives on Human Dignity and Human Rights: An Introduction* (2022); Sean T. Dempsey, *City of Dignity: Christianity, Liberalism, and the Making of Global Los Angeles* (2022); Clemens Sedmak, *Enacting Catholic Social Tradition: The Deep Practice of Human Dignity* (2022); Aimee Byrd, *The Sexual Reformation: Restoring the Dignity and Personhood of Man and Woman* (2022); Matthew R. Petrusek, *Value and Vulnerability: An Interfaith Dialogue on Human Dignity* (2020); Anne-Marie Dillens and Bernard Van Meenen, *Dignity Today: Philosophical and Theological Perspectives* (2019); Murray Joseph Casey, "Value-Based Costing of Anti-cancer Drugs: An Ethical Perspective Grounded in Catholic Teachings on Human Dignity and the Common Good," *Issues in Law and Medicine* 36 (2021): 44. In 2021, *Brigham Young University Law School* dedicated volume 46:5 to *Human Dignity and Human Rights— Christian Perspectives and Practices: A Focus on Constitutional and International Law.*

[k] Dignity philosophy and ethics include Mokphi Chikh, *Discourse on Universalism and Human Dignity: The Enlightened Individual* (2024); Michael Wainwright, *Kantian Dignity and Trolley Problems in the Literature of Richard Wright* (2024); Nayef R. F. Al-Rodhan, *Sustainable History and Human Dignity: A Neurophilosophy of History and the Future of Civilisation* (2022); Jan-Willem van der Rijt and Adam Steven Cureton, *Human Dignity and the Kingdom of*

Finally, we come to the books about dignity and law. The majority of these (by my very unofficial count) are about dignity and human rights law. This makes sense, since the idea of dignity as a legal concept comes to us through the 1945 Charter of the United Nations and the 1948 Universal Declaration of Human Rights and has been developed by their progeny at international, regional, and national levels. While everyone seems to accept that dignity is the axis around which the regime of human rights revolves, it has eluded precise definition, and this seems to invite abundant academic elucidation. A few of the most recent examples are noted below. Some of these are on specific aspects of human rights, such as technology and bioethics,[1]

Ends: Kantian Perspectives and Practical Applications (2022); Suzy Killmister, *Contours of Dignity* (2020); Jean Claude Bisimwa, *Respect as the Foundation of a Sustainable Society: Humanity in Me, Humanity in Others* (2019); Richard Berquist, *From Human Dignity to Natural Law: An Introduction* (2019); Stephan Leher, *Dignity and Human Rights: Language, Philosophy, and Social Realizations* (2018); John Douglas Macready, *Hannah Arendt and the Fragility of Human Dignity* (2018); Austin Sarat, Antonio Pele, and Stephen Riley, *Human Dignity* (2022); Anthony Ekanem, *Living with Dignity: How to Treat People as You Would Like Them to Treat You* (2022); Andani Thakhathi, *Transcendent Development: The Ethics of Universal Dignity* (2022); Michał Rupniewski, *Human Dignity and the Law: A Personalist Theory* (2022); Marco Ettore Grasso, *The Ontological Maze: Ethics, Dignity, and the Critical Essences of Identity and Sustainability* (2024).

[1] See, for instance, Michael Casey and Frank H. McCourt, *Our Biggest Fight: Reclaiming Liberty, Humanity, and Dignity in the Digital Age* (2024); Marcello Ienca, Oreste Pollicino, and Laura Liguori, *The Cambridge Handbook of Information Technology, Life Sciences, and Human Rights* (2022); Dan Saxon, *Fighting Machines: Autonomous Weapons and Human Dignity* (2022); Danielle Keats Citron, *The Fight for Privacy: Protecting Dignity, Identity, and Love in the Dig-*

democracy,[m] criminal law,[n] economics,[o] or immigration.[p] Some books narrow the gaze and use dignity as a focal point

---

ital Age (2022); Ro Khanna, *Dignity in a Digital Age: Making Tech Work for All of Us* (2022); Brigitte Feuillet-Liger and Kristina Orfali, eds., *The Reality of Human Dignity in Law and Bioethics: Comparative Perspectives* (2018); Virginia Kozemczak, "Dignity, Freedom, and Digital Rights: Comparing American and European Approaches to Privacy," *Cardozo International and Comparative Law Review* 4 (2021): 1069; Evangelos D. Protopapadakis, *Creating Unique Copies: Human Reproductive Cloning, Uniqueness, and Dignity* (2023).

[m] Mario Krešić, Damir Banović, Alberto Carrio Sampedro, and J. Pleps, *Ethnic Diversity, Plural Democracy and Human Dignity: Challenges to the European Union and Western Balkans* (2022); Daniel Bedford, Catherine Dupré, Gábor Halmai, and Panos Kapotas, *Human Dignity and Democracy in Europe: Synergies, Tensions and Crises* (2022).

[n] Books about dignity in the criminal law include Sylvain Niquège, *The Dispute over the Dignity of Detention Conditions* (2023); Erin Daly, *Dignity in the Criminal Legal System: A Policy Guide for Advocacy and Reform* (2024); Judge Victoria Pratt, *The Power of Dignity: How Transforming Justice Can Heal Our Communities* (2022). See also James Park Taylor, "Through a Glass Darkly: Cruel & Unusual Punishment Clause Examined through the Lens of the Right to Dignity," *Montana Law Review* 46 (2021): 18; James Park Taylor, "Intersection of Hybrid Rights: Dignity and Protection against Excessive Punishment," *Montana Law Review* 46 (2021): 20; Ben A. McJunkin, "Ensuring Dignity as Public Safety," *American Criminal Law Review* 59 (2022): 1643; Victoria Pratt, "Why Dignity and Respect Matter in Our Courts," *Litigation* 48 (2022): 27.

[o] Books about economics and dignity include David Buckham, Robyn Wilkinson, and Christiaan Straeuli, *The Age of Menace: Capitalism, Inequality & the Battle for Dignity* (2022); Hugues Puel, *Paths of Humanism: Building Dignity; Undertaking Innovations* (2019); Chrystin Ondersma, *Dignity Not Debt: An Abolitionist Approach to Economic Justice* (2024) [focusing on personal debt in America].

[p] Anna Lise Purkey, *Refugee Dignity in Protracted Exile* (2021).

for discussion about gender,[q] race,[r] or other specific topics of

---

[q] Books about women, men, gender, and dignity include Ann Cart-
wright, *Dignity of Labour? A Study of Childbearing and Induction*
[originally published in 1979, republished in 2024]; Myanda Klaark,
F . . . like Human (2022); Lilian Chudey Pride, *Dignity of Woman-
hood* (2022); Alice Gerlach, *Dignity, Women, and Immigration
Detention* (2022). See also Anna High, "Sexual Dignity and Rape
Law," *Yale Journal of Law & Feminism* 33 (2022): 1; Andrew S. Park,
"Respecting LGBTQ Dignity through Vital Capabilities," *Journal of
Gender Race & Justice* 24 (2021): 271.
    There are a number of books and law review articles about dig-
nity and menstruation in particular: Celeste Mergens, *The Power
of Days: A Story of Resilience, Dignity, and the Fight for Women's
Equity* (2023); Marcy L. Karin, Margaret E. Johnson, and Eliza-
beth B. Cooper, "Menstrual Dignity and the Bar Exam," *UC Davis
Law Review* 55 (2021): 1; Elizabeth B. Cooper, "What's Law Got to
Do with It? Dignity and Menstruation," *Columbia Journal of Gender
and Law* 41 (2021): 39; Amy Fettig, "Menstrual Equity, Organizing,
and the Struggle for Human Dignity and Gender Equality in Prison,"
Columbia Journal of Gender and Law 41 (2021): 76.

[r] Books that use dignity as a lens for examining racial conflicts, ethnicity, indigeneity, and identity include Danielle Z. Boles, *Towards
Dignity in Health: From Health-White Associations to the Recla-
mation of Racial-Ethnic Minority Cultures of Health* (2023); Marta
Padovan-Ozdemir and Trine Oland, *Racism in Danish Welfare
Work with Refugees: Troubled by Difference, Docility and Dignity*
(2022); Madhulina Bandyopadhyay, *Yes to Dignity: A Journey to Un-
slavery through the Dirty White Ceiling of Federal Reserve* (2022);
Vincent W. Lloyd, *Black Dignity: The Struggle against Domination*
(2022); Norman Ajari, *Dignity or Death: Ethics and Politics of Race*
(2019); Muriel Cuissard, *Clothing in the Hip-Hop Movement: Em-
powerment and Dignity* (2019). See also Bill Piatt, "Respecting the
Identity and Dignity of All Indigenous Americans," *Howard Human
& Civil Rights Law Review* 6 (2021–2022): 83; Cody Uyeda, "Mountains, Telescopes, and Broken Promises: The Dignity Taking of Ha-
waii's Ceded Lands," *Asian American Law Journal* 28 (2021): 65;

attention.[s] Others investigate the place of dignity in human rights theory and practice more broadly.[t]

John Felipe Acevedo, "Reclaiming Black Dignity," *Texas Law Review Online* 99 (2020–2021): 1.

[s] For instance, there are several books about dignity and disability, including Julia Duffy, *Mental Capacity, Dignity and the Power of International Human Rights* (2023); Linda Barclay, *Disability with Dignity: Justice, Human Rights and Equal Status* (2020).

[t] Books about dignity in the center of human rights practice and theory include Aniceto Masferrer, *The Making of Dignity and Human Rights in the Western Tradition: A Retrospective Analysis* (2024); Glen T. Martin, *Human Dignity and World Order: The Holistic Foundations of Global Democracy* (2024); Boris Barraud, *Dignity, Freedom, Equality: Practice of Human Rights* (2022); Pablo Gilabert, *Human Dignity and Human Rights* (2019) and *Human Dignity and Social Justice* (2023); Brett G. Scharffs and Ewelina U. Ochab, *Dignity and International Human Rights Law: An Introduction to the Punta del Este Declaration on Human Dignity for Everyone Everywhere* (2022); J. M. Aroso Linhares, *Human Dignity and the Autonomy of Law* (2022); Salvador Santino F. Regilme Jr. and Irene Hadiprayitno, eds., *Human Rights at Risk: Global Governance, American Power, and the Future of Dignity* (2022); Mary V. Alfred, Petra A. Robinson, and Elizabeth A. Roumell, eds., *Advancing the Global Agenda for Human Rights, Vulnerable Populations, and Environmental Sustainability* (2021); Andrea Gattini, Rosana Garciandia, and Philippa Webb, eds., *Human Dignity and International Law* (2021); Ginevra Le Moli, *Human Dignity in International Law* (2021); Angus J. L. Menuge, *The Inherence of Human Dignity: Foundations of Human Dignity, Volume 1* and *Law and Religious Liberty, Volume 2* (2021); Zhibin Xie, Pauline Kollontai, and Sebastian Kim., eds., *Human Dignity, Human Rights, and Social Justice: A Chinese Interdisciplinary Dialogue with Global Perspective* (2020); Hoda Mahmoudi, *Interdisciplinary Perspectives on Human Dignity and Human Rights* (2019); Matthew McManus, *Making Human Dignity Central to International Human Rights Law: A Critical Legal Argument* (2019); Amós Nascimento and Matthias Lutz-Bachmann,

A small number focus on the cases themselves.[u] Only Rachel Bayevsky's book, *Dignity and Judicial Authority,* along with some law review articles, focuses on American law. Some of the latter address issues of particular importance in the United States such as freedom of speech,[v] and for a time, the use of dignity in the jurisprudence of Justice Kennedy, particularly in cases involving same-sex relations.[w] Though I have contributed to this scholarship, I have not relied on these articles extensively

---

eds., *Human Dignity: Perspectives from a Critical Theory of Human Rights* (2018); Elaine Webster, *Dignity, Degrading Treatment and Torture in Human Rights Law: The Ends of Article 3 of the European Convention on Human Rights* (2018). See also David Hollenbach, "A Relational Understanding of Human Rights: Human Dignity in Social Solidarity," *Emory Law Journal* 71 (2022): 1487.

[u] Brett G. Scharffs, Andrea Pin, D. Vovk, and M. V. Antonov, *Human Dignity, Judicial Reasoning, and the Law: Comparative Perspectives on a Key Constitutional Concept* (2024); Rachel Bayefsky, *Dignity and Judicial Authority* (2024).

[v] Jason Zenor, "A Private Practice? Commercial Speech, Public Accommodation, and Individual Dignity," *Elon Law Review* 14 (2022): 87; Raphael Cohen-Almagor, "Taking Profound Offence Seriously: Freedom of Speech v. Human Dignity," *Journal of Hate Studies* 16 (2020): 1.

[w] See, e.g., John G. Roberts, "In Tribute: Justice Anthony M. Kennedy," *Harvard Law Review* 132 (2018): 1; Eric J. Scarffe, "Justice Kennedy's Jurisprudence of Dignity: From Sovereign Immunity to Gay Rights," *American Journal of Legal History* 63, no. 4 (December 2023): 359–380; Adeno Addis, "Justice Kennedy on Dignity," *Houston Law Review* 52 (2015): 825; Laurence H. Tribe, "Equal Dignity: Speaking Its Name," *Harvard Law Review* 129 (2015): 28; Kenji Yoshino, "A New Birth of Freedom? *Obergefell v. Hodges,*" *Harvard Law Review* 129 (2015): 147; Tobin Sparling, "A Path Unfollowed: The Disregard of Dignity Precedent in Justice Kennedy's Jurisprudence," *Tulane Law Review* 93 (2018): 115.

in this book for two reasons. First, the aim of this book is not jurisprudential analysis, so I have not dipped deeply into the legal literature on any of the issues discussed in this book. Second, I think that Justice Kennedy's commitment to dignity created a beautiful opening for the law to reflect the values I espouse here, and for that reason, it garnered a lot of attention when the cases were coming out; however, even in these cases, Justice Kennedy did not explore or develop what he meant by dignity and why it should be embedded in our constitutional law. I believe that if he had, our constitutional law would be much better and stronger, and the issues I have discussed in this book would already have a strong dignity foundation. As it happens, his departure from the Court ended that dalliance with dignity, and none of the justices presently on the court seem likely to revisit it.

For most of the literature, the vast majority assumes or argues that human dignity is an appropriate, or the most appropriate, touchstone for addressing important social matters. As Carrie Booth Walling writes in *Human Rights and Justice for All,* "This book is about the powerful idea of human rights and the belief that all people are equally deserving of dignity and rights. . . . We can advance human rights by placing the well-being and dignity of other human beings at the center of the decisions we make personally and as a community."[x] In *Human Dignity and World Order: The Holistic Foundations of Global Democracy,* Glen T. Martin writes, "We need a world system *predicated on* human dignity and the right to peace. This is our central and most fundamental option for making possible any credible future at all for humanity"[y]. No small order. Some books seem to use it as a stand-in for justice, whether economic justice or some other

---

[x] Carrie Booth Walling, *Human Rights and Justice for All: Demanding Dignity in the United States and around the World* (2022).

[y] Glen T. Martin, Human Dignity and World Order: The Holistic Foundations of Global Democracy (2024), at 32.

kind, such as Harlan Beckley's *Rethinking Equal Opportunity: Dignity, Human Capability, and Justice* (2024), which uses the concept of dignity to connect to equal economic opportunity.

Of all of these, I found Matthew McManus's book, *Making Human Dignity Central to International Human Rights Law: A Critical Legal Argument*, especially interesting because it examines in depth what the word entails and how it may be applied. He conceives of dignity as "dignified self-authorship" centered on an individual's "ability to reject and transform the false necessity of the socio-historical context within which they live."[z]

In two important senses, this is related to Mark Coleman's conception of dignity and aligns with the way global jurisprudence uses and applies dignity and with the way I have used it in this book. First, it is relational. It is the flipside of Sartre's notion in *No Exit* that "hell is other people." For McManus and Coleman, as with the African conception of ubuntu, only in our relations with other people do we find our own dignity. McManus explains in the section "Dignity and Expressive Capabilities": "I reject the idea . . . that dignity is somehow an inherent quality enjoyed by all. Instead, I accept the claims of the relational school that dignity depends on the relations that individuals are capable of establishing in the world, and the myriad ways in which they are able to operationalize their agency to engage in dignified self-authorship."

McManus rejects the inherence thesis in part because if dignity is inherent, then it can't be social, and if it isn't social, then it's irrelevant to law. But this is a false duality, as the cases on which I have relied reveal. In these cases, dignity is both inherent

---

[z] Matthew McManus, *Making Human Dignity Central to International Human Rights Law: A Critical Legal Argument* (2019), passim, and at 56.

in the individual *and* relational, precisely because individuals necessarily need relationships. And relationships need individuals. With the exception of Justice Clarence Thomas (as discussed at the end of Chapter 1), judges around the world think that law is necessary to protect the inherent worth of every person, and they have fashioned an extensive and globally coherent body of case law that reflects this.

Second, some of these authors focus on dignity precisely because of its transformative potential. This is its near-explicit function in the UN Charter and the Universal Declaration of Human Rights. Remember, the UN Charter begins with the following:

WE THE PEOPLES OF THE UNITED NATIONS DETERMINED

to save succeeding generations from the scourge of war, which twice in our lifetime has brought untold sorrow to mankind, and

to reaffirm faith in fundamental human rights, in the dignity and worth of the human person, in the equal rights of men and women and of nations large and small.[aa]

The transformational power of dignity is evident in the instruments and constitutions that have followed and that support the claim that we live in the "Age of Dignity," to use Catherine Dupré's evocative phrase.[ab] At a personal level, the idea of transformation finds resonance, too, in Hannah Arendt's observation that only human beings have the capacity for rebirth and redefining their lives, and also in Mark Coleman's suggestion (noted earlier) that the concept of dignity can transform the relationships one has with other individuals and with society as a whole.

[aa] Charter of the United Nations, preamble.

[ab] Catherine Dupré, *The Age of Dignity: Human Rights and Constitutionalism in Europe* (2015).

Marco Ettore Grasso's *The Ontological Maze: Ethics, Dignity, and the Critical Essences of Identity and Sustainability* similarly "presents itself as a new transformative-emancipatory path,"[ac] and Martin in *Human Dignity and World Order: The Holistic Foundations of Global Democracy* seeks to use dignity to unlock the "utopian imagination." Dignity's transformational power has certainly not been lost on the courts, and it animates the central argument made in this book.

However, some books are already lamenting the dimming of the light of dignity. In *Lost Dignity*, Christian Hein examines in great detail the hypocrisy of the West in, on the one hand, making human dignity "the ultimate category of *self-reference* for Western cultural systems by which they reflect and coordinate themselves and their actions" and, on the other, being responsible for vast and deep violations of dignity in domestic and international policy.[ad] Orit Kamir has a different take: In *Betraying Dignity: The Toxic Seduction of Social Media, Shaming, and Radicalization*, she argues that "in the second decade of the twenty-first century, many people around the world are fleeing the social and political culture established less than a century ago, after two world wars, which [she calls] a dignity-based culture. As we abandon this new culture, we return to an older cultural structure that has been around for millennia, which, following anthropologists, [she calls] an honor-based culture."[ae] The book is full of profound insights and connections that have

---

[ac] Marco Ettore Grasso, *The Ontological Maze: Ethics, Dignity and the Critical Essences of Identity and Sustainability* (2024), https://www.peterlang.com/document/1418486.

[ad] Christian Hein, *Lost Dignity* (2023), 13.

[ae] Orit Kamir, *Betraying Dignity: The Toxic Seduction of Social Media, Shaming, and Radicalization* (2019), xi.

eluded the attention of many others, even though they are star-
ing us in the face. Briefly, the argument is this:

> Overwhelming change and uncertainty that plague the turn of
> the twenty-first century have shaken the proclaimed universal
> allegiance to human dignity and rights. In times of upheaval and
> uncertainty, dignity apparently seems too thin, abstract, and im-
> personal to many people around the globe. They feel lonely and
> unprotected in the face of devastating changes. This leads many to
> see comfort and safety in traditional social systems based on honor.
> Yet they find that there is no going back to severed primordial ties
> and no rekindling of traditional, organic honor-based clans, tribes,
> and extended families. The fear of existence in a world based on
> individualist dignity, enhanced by the longing for the imagined
> comforts and warmth of a collectivistic world based on honor, has
> been directing people to follow two new paths. One of these paths
> recommends authoritarian, semitotalitarian, social orders, estab-
> lished and run by populist, neo-fascist, or fundamentalist parties
> and leaders. . . . The other path leads to the arms of all-consuming
> virtual social media, to virtual versions of Islam or to the identity
> politics of victimhood culture.[af]

Kamir describes "a fear of life under human dignity-based
culture and the consequential flight from it" toward "new, patho-
logical versions of honor-based culture."[ag] I found this book to be
quite compelling, and it resonates in what I called in the Preface the politics of fear. I suppose the present book is an effort to
reassert the commitment to a dignity-based culture, at least in
America.

One last book I want to mention is Steven Hitlin and Matthew A. Andersson's *The Science of Dignity: Measuring Personhood and Well-Being in the United States* (2023). This is part of
a growing literature that takes dignity into the realm of public

---

[af] Kamir, *Betraying Dignity*, 4.

[ag] Kamir, *Betraying Dignity*, 2.

health. It seeks to measure people's own sense of their dignity and correlate that with people's health and well-being. After a very broad review of the various claims about the meaning of dignity and various moments in history and in various fields of inquiry, the authors settle on their own definition, which involves three Ms: mastery, or a sense of control over one's life; mission, or a sense of purpose in one's life; and mattering, that is, in relation to others. You can see how these align with the definitions of dignity that derive from the case law and that I have used throughout the book.

I am gratified to see this burgeoning scholarship around the theme of human dignity and excited to see where it takes us next.

Index

The authorized representative in the EU for product safety and compliance is:
Mare Nostrum Group
B.V Doelen 72
4831 GR Breda
The Netherlands

www.ingramcontent.com/pod-product-compliance
Lightning Source LLC
Chambersburg PA
CBHW021924190326
41519CB00009B/900